GO ASK AUSTEN

LIFE LESSONS *from* JANE AUSTEN

GO ASK AUSTEN

LIFE LESSONS *from* JANE AUSTEN

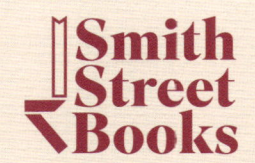

Smith Street Books

CONTENTS

Introduction	6
How to spot a true gentleman by his estate	8
What to do when you despise your friend's love interest	18
What your birth order says about you	26
How to be a memorable letter writer	34
Convalescing after an ill-conceived stroll in the rain	44
Embarrassing things your family does, ranked	52
An introvert's guide to balls	60
What to do when you are this week's gossip	70
What to consider before saying "yes"	78
Signs he's a rake you (and your sisters) should avoid	86
Things only true friends understand	96
Types of acquaintances every circle must have	104
Unexpected places to secure a suitor	112
Must-have items to spend your pin money on	122
Hobbies that are better than matchmaking	130
Truths that are universally acknowledged	138

Introduction

It is a truth universally acknowledged that Jane Austen is one of the greatest writers of all time. She left us with six complete masterpieces—*Sense and Sensibility* (1811), *Pride and Prejudice* (1813), *Mansfield Park* (1814), *Emma* (1815), and *Persuasion* and *Northanger Abbey* (both published posthumously in 1817). Well after her death, her *Juvenilia*, the unfinished manuscripts *The Watsons* and *Sanditon*, and *Lady Susan*, an epistolary novel, were all eventually published.

Within these works is a bounty of sparkling characters and heartwarming stories, full of witty and wise insights on only the most important things—love, friendship, family, society, economics, and, of course, fashion. Whilst her stories are *the* blueprint for the romantic comedy genre, her words also offer a blueprint for life. Which is what you'll find within the pages of this book—a guide to living your best life, as inspired by Austen and the wonderful characters she gave us.

Hopefully it will help you find answers to that ever-relevant question: What would Austen do?

How to Spot a True Gentleman by His Estate

(It's not just size that matters.)

A visit to a gentleman's home is a chance to glean insight into his character, particularly when the opportunity arises to visit the residence of a person you recently declared to be arrogant and conceited. While calling upon potential and prior suitors, here is a list of details around his estate to keep note of :

➤ IT IS WELL KEPT

A true gentleman keeps his home and surrounds immaculate. Or, at the very least, he employs an extensive staff to do so.

➤ HIS HOUSEHOLD IS CONTENT

You can always judge a gentleman by how well he treats those who work for him. If he is rude or does not offer fair conditions, he is not of sound character.

➤ HIS TENANTS ARE CONTENT *See above.*

➤ IT YIELDS A HEARTY INCOME

One must have something to live on. A mere few thousand a year and at least two carriages are not too much to ask.

➤ THERE ARE MANY WINDOWS

A necessity for light and, indeed, daily life. Additionally, they allow you to admire your domain—that is, *ahem*, his domain.

➤ THERE IS AN EXTENSIVE LIBRARY

A gentleman should have a keen appreciation of the importance of growing his library, regardless of whether he plans to read a single volume.

➤ IT IS TASTEFULLY DECORATED

Good taste in furnishings, as in all aspects of life, is vital. Even if the gentleman in question did inherit all his possessions from his great-great-great-grandparents.

➤ THERE IS A LAKE

A place for your uncle to fish, perhaps ... or for a gentleman to take a refreshing swim in his underclothes. Not that you would ever think of such things. No.

A HEROINE WHO NEEDS NO INTRODUCTION

ELIZABETH BENNET

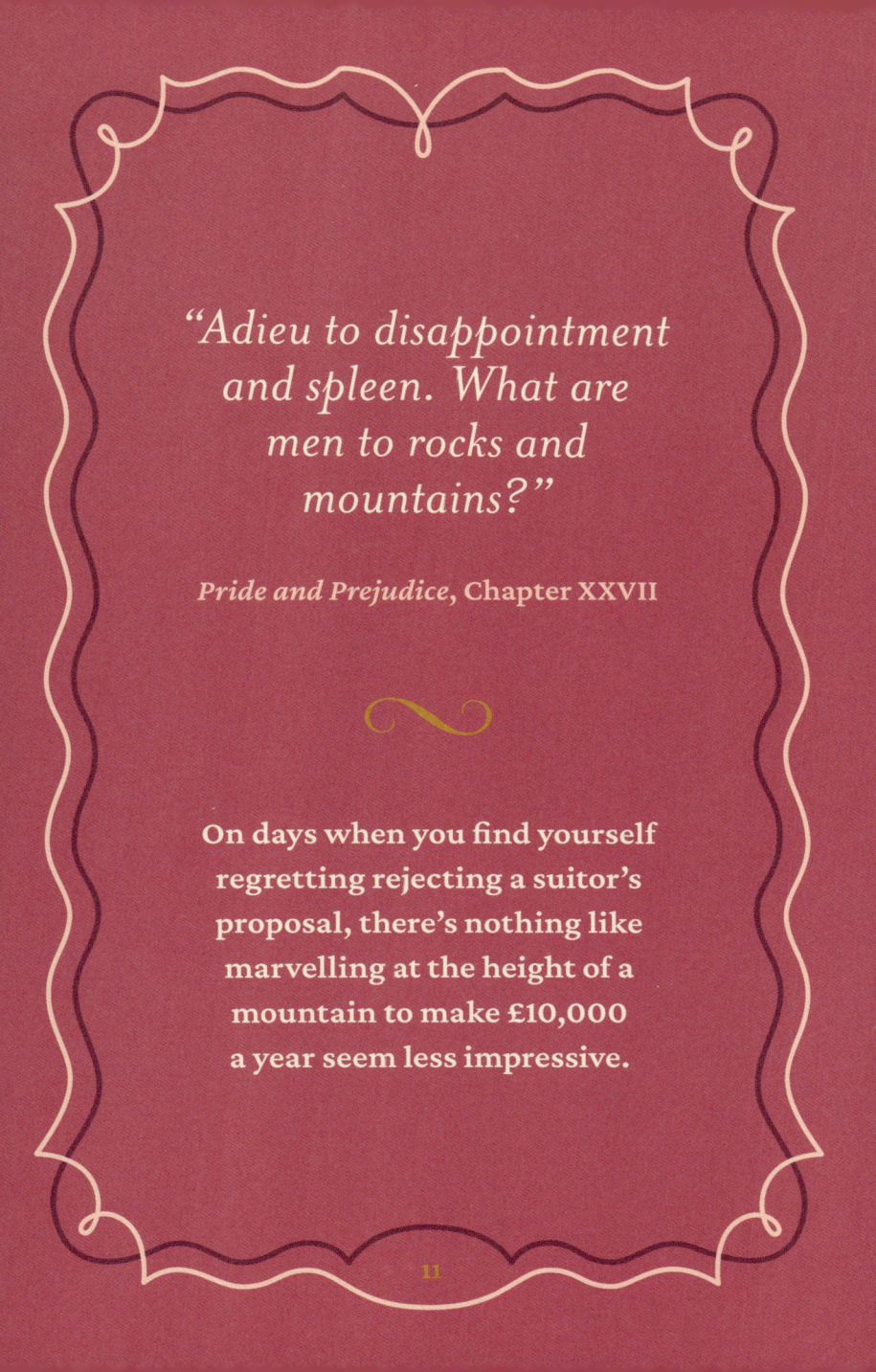

"Adieu to disappointment and spleen. What are men to rocks and mountains?"

Pride and Prejudice, Chapter XXVII

On days when you find yourself regretting rejecting a suitor's proposal, there's nothing like marvelling at the height of a mountain to make £10,000 a year seem less impressive.

FANNY PRICE'S MORE UNPLEASANT AUNT

MRS NORRIS

"And remember that, if you are ever so forward and clever yourselves, you should always be modest; for, much as you know already, there is a great deal more for you to learn."

Mansfield Park, Chapter II

∽

While you may have mastered music, singing, dancing, and all the modern languages, a truly accomplished person does not brag about their talents.

A GENTLEMAN WITH A TRAGIC PAST

COLONEL BRANDON

> "… and yet there is something so amiable in the prejudices of a young mind, that one is sorry to see them give way to the reception of more general opinions."

Sense and Sensibility, Chapter XI

Being correct is not always the best route to happiness.

CATHERINE MORLAND'S
STEADFAST FRIEND

ISABELLA THORPE

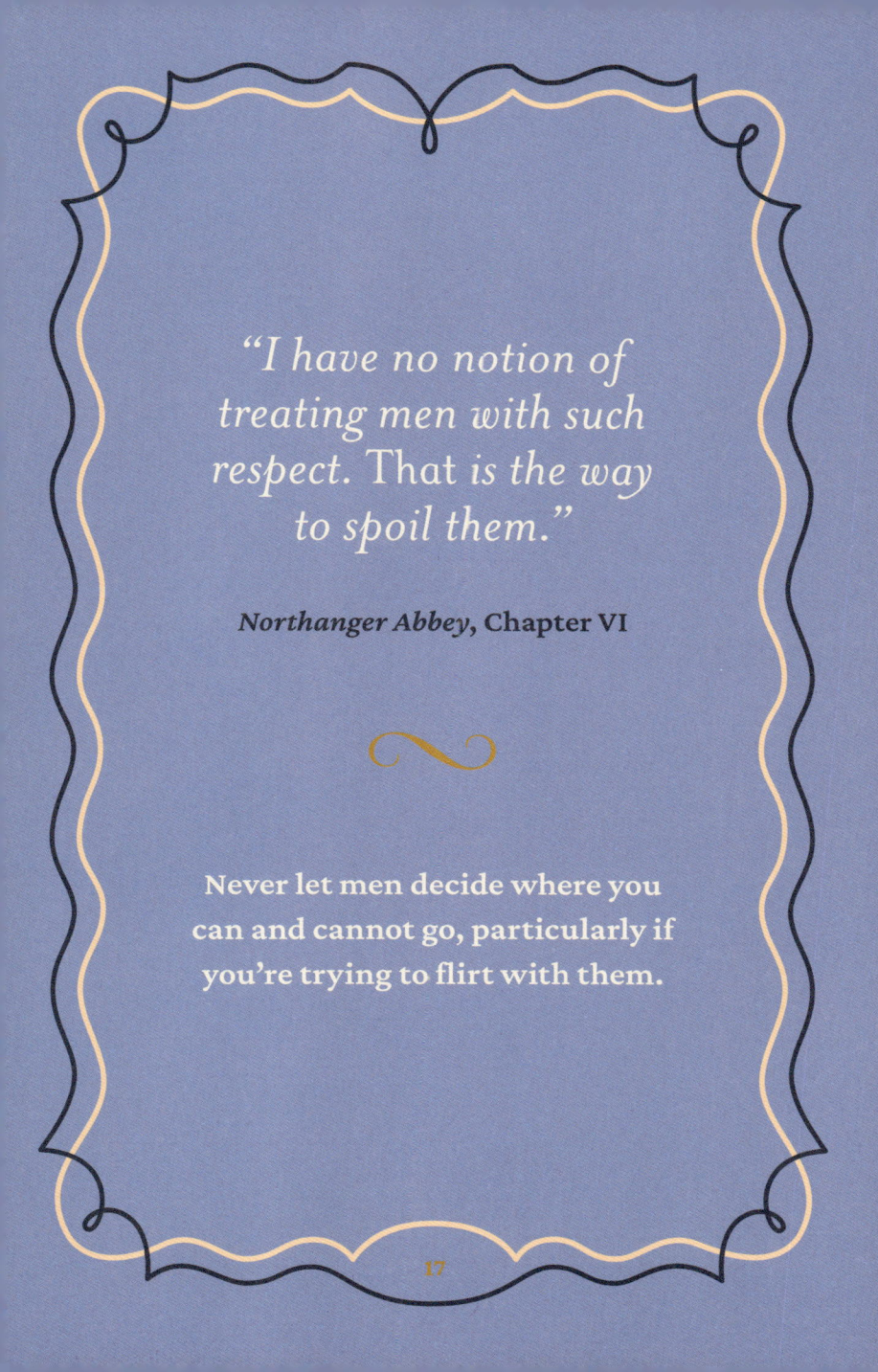

"I have no notion of treating men with such respect. That *is* the way to spoil them."

Northanger Abbey, **Chapter VI**

Never let men decide where you can and cannot go, particularly if you're trying to flirt with them.

What to Do When You Despise Your Friend's Love Interest

There is little in this world that poses a greater threat to a friend's happiness than an ill-suited match. As their close companion, it's your duty to safeguard them (and your enjoyment of visiting their house) from misplaced affections. And so, a proposal to avoid much unhappiness for all parties:

- Explain to your friend why this match would be ill-suited.
- Grow cross when your friend doesn't take your wisdom and advice seriously.
- Work with your friend's siblings to make the strongest case for your friend's lack of clarity.
- Gaslight your friend into thinking the object of their affections actually cares very little for them.
- Intercept any correspondence so that your friend believes the object of their affections has disappeared without a trace, and vice versa.
- Pursue your own undesirable and unsuitable match with a sibling of your friend's love interest, despite the hypocrisy of such actions.
- Be rejected and have an existential crisis.
- Realise the error of your ways and do everything you can to remedy them.
- Help your friend reunite with their love interest, so that you may get together with yours.
- Have a double wedding and settle near each other.
- Alternatively, do none of the above and simply offer your friend tactful opinions and advice, but ultimately respect their wishes.
- Unless, of course, your friend is marrying the endlessly grateful holder of the living near your wealthy and esteemed aunt. In which case, perhaps encourage them to finally go on that Grand Tour they've been discussing.

THE ELDEST OF THE BERTRAM SIBLINGS

TOM BERTRAM

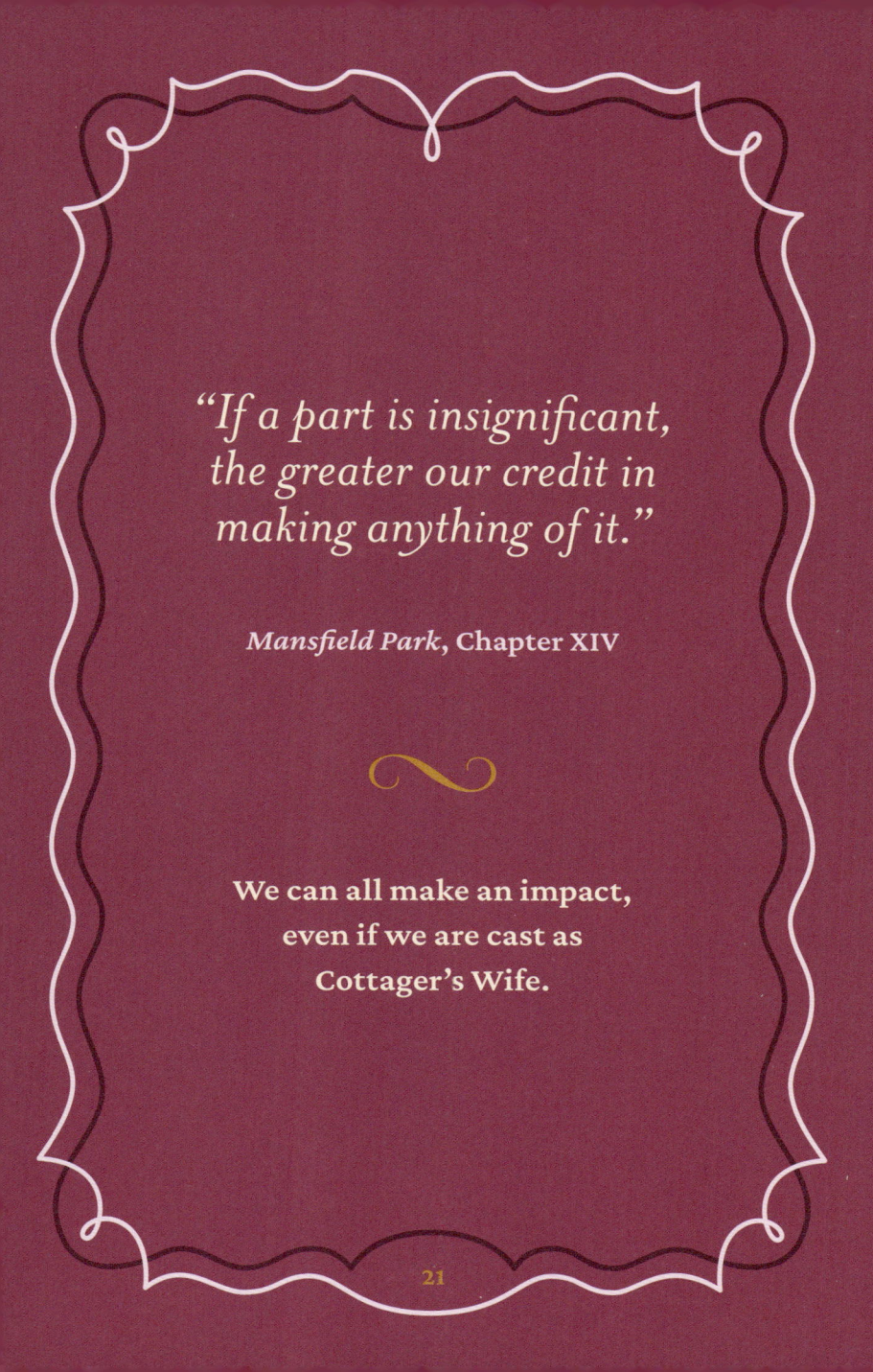

> "If a part is insignificant, the greater our credit in making anything of it."

Mansfield Park, Chapter XIV

We can all make an impact, even if we are cast as Cottager's Wife.

NARRATOR

EMMA

"Seldom, very seldom, does complete truth belong to any human disclosure; seldom can it happen that something is not a little disguised, or a little mistaken …"

Emma, Chapter XIII

Avoid assuming your crush
is in love with your friend
until you've confirmed they
are wearing a lock of their hair.

ELINOR DASHWOOD'S UNDERSTATED SUITOR

Edward Ferrars

"I am not fond of nettles or thistles, or heath blossoms. I have more pleasure in a snug farm-house than a watch-tower—and a troop of tidy, happy villagers please me better than the finest banditti in the world."

Sense and Sensibility, Chapter XVIII

We each deserve to pursue our own happiness, whether that's by sailing the high seas or idling on a sofa.

What Your Birth Order Says About You

There are few who can know one better than one's siblings. You share a home, a room, and sometimes even attention from the same member of the militia. From title to personality, however, siblings' inheritances diverge, dictated by whether they are the oldest or one of four middle children. Here is a brief study of the effects birth order has upon temperament:

THE ELDEST

For those born first, there is a pressure to be the most beautiful and accomplished—so it is a good thing that is exactly what you are. It is up to you, after all, to set a fine path for your siblings. You are your parents' experiment, doomed to suffer the ill effects of their inexperience with none of the coddling your younger siblings are gifted. As such, you are resilient and wise beyond your years, with a large emotional capacity and cutting wit. Because sometimes, if you do not laugh, you shall cry, and one must do what one can to avoid an unbecomingly swollen face.

THE MIDDLE

For better or worse, the eldest and the youngest in families tend to get the most attention, leaving you rather forgotten. Sometimes it gets a little lonely, but most of the time you are glad to be left to your own devices—you are quite independent and resourceful, and it gives you the chance to master the pianoforte. But you are also very considerate of the feelings of others; you know all too well how it feels to have your own trampled on constantly. Your time to shine will come—even if you must give your siblings a little push out of the spotlight and into marriage to get it.

THE YOUNGEST

Your parents were so busy and exhausted by the time you came along, you benefitted from what may best be described as benign neglect. That is, you have received plenty of adoration and attention but very few boundaries. Consequently, you virtually always get your way. You live to enjoy yourself and help others have fun—you are the life of the ball. Unfortunately, you also tend to be impatient and impulsive, which, paired with a somewhat inflated ego and lack of self-awareness, can have disastrous consequences. Never mind—it's nothing that cannot be remedied with a good social disgrace or two. Just be mindful of men who mention they've always wanted to visit Gretna Green.

THE ELDEST BENNET SISTER

JANE BENNET

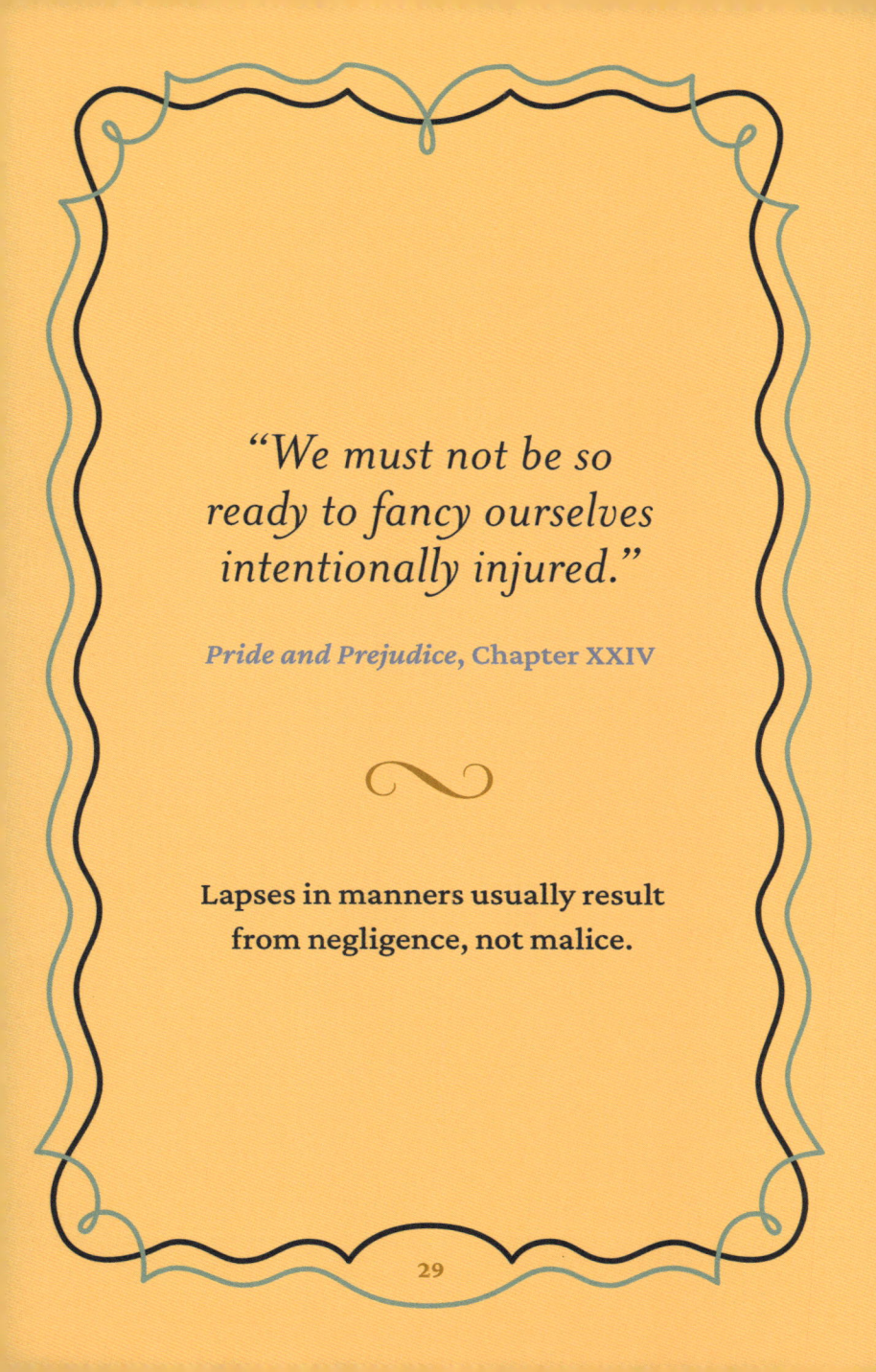

"We must not be so ready to fancy ourselves intentionally injured."

Pride and Prejudice, **Chapter XXIV**

∽

Lapses in manners usually result from negligence, not malice.

CAPTAIN WENTWORTH'S
BROTHER-IN-LAW

Admiral Croft

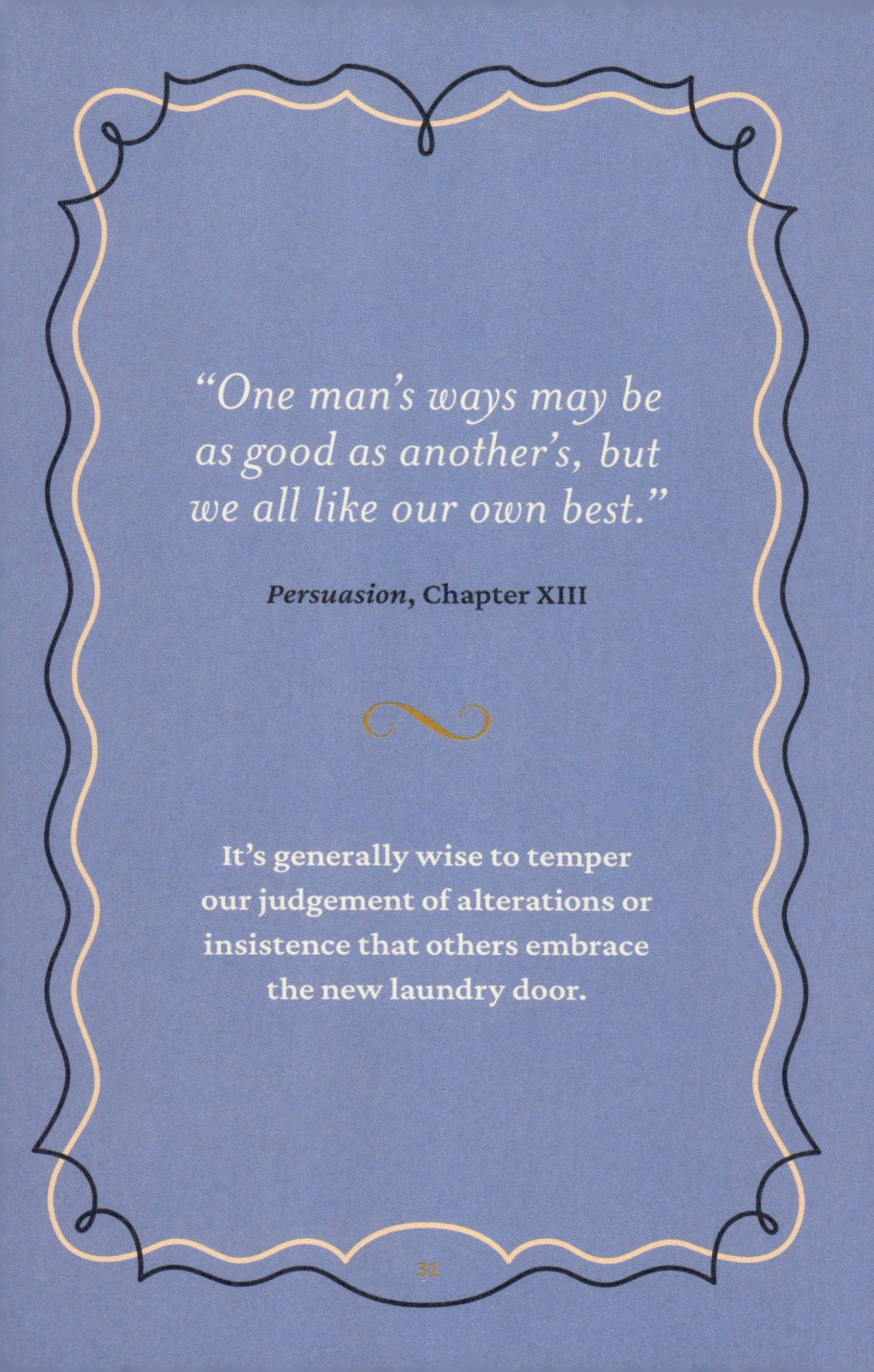

"One man's ways may be as good as another's, but we all like our own best."

Persuasion, Chapter XIII

It's generally wise to temper our judgement of alterations or insistence that others embrace the new laundry door.

**A FRIEND OF THE BERTRAMS
AND AN ENEMY OF THE CLERGY**

MARY CRAWFORD

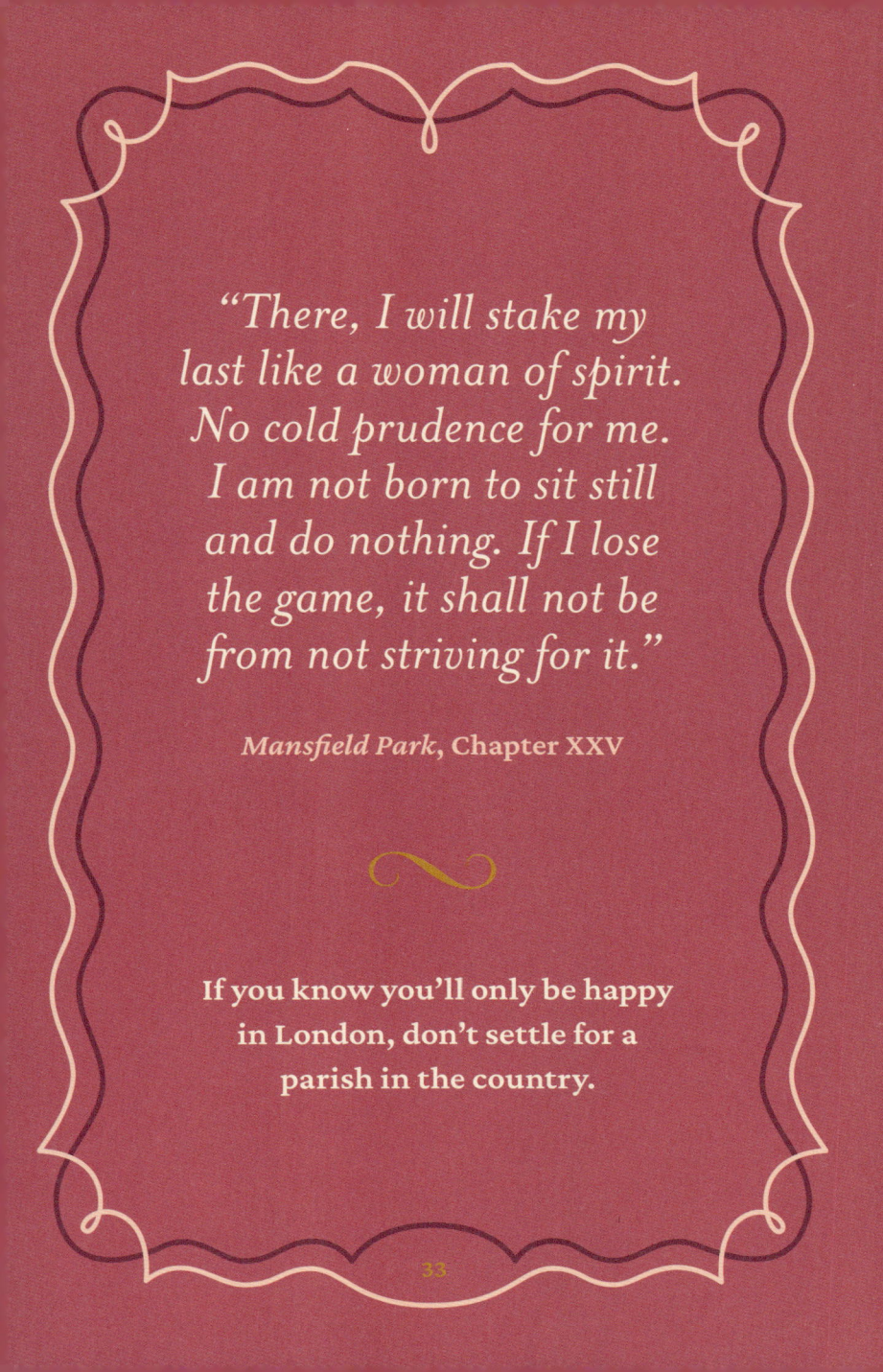

"There, I will stake my last like a woman of spirit. No cold prudence for me. I am not born to sit still and do nothing. If I lose the game, it shall not be from not striving for it."

Mansfield Park, Chapter XXV

If you know you'll only be happy in London, don't settle for a parish in the country.

How to be a Memorable Letter Writer

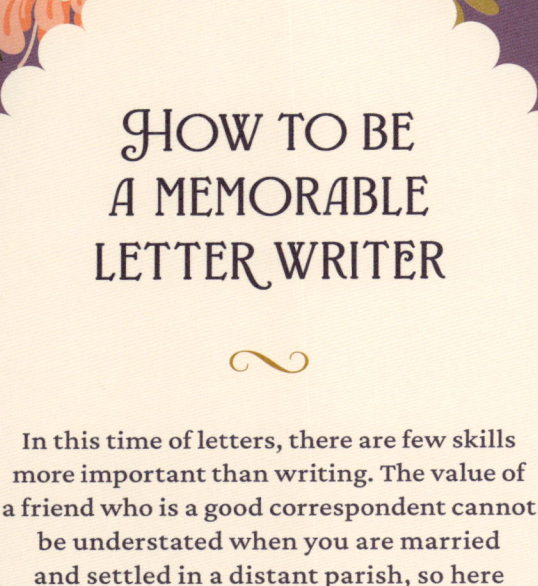

In this time of letters, there are few skills more important than writing. The value of a friend who is a good correspondent cannot be understated when you are married and settled in a distant parish, so here is some advice to ensure you continue to receive frequent responses:

➤ KNOW YOUR AUDIENCE

Is your recipient a close friend or mere acquaintance? Will they guard all your secrets? Even destroy your letters, if that is what is best? Or are they likely to share their contents? And do you want them to? The answers to such questions will entirely dictate the content of your writing and exactly how many of your neighbours' names you mention.

➤ CHOOSE YOUR TOPIC

Is this a simple life update (acceptable, if there is nothing else on offer) or do you have something more exciting to divulge? Perhaps a declaration of love, disguised as a riddle? Remember that the recipient will have to pay for your letter, after all. Make it worth their pennies. Avoid boring them with dull details such as the cost of a neighbour's window glazing. Unless, of course, your recipient is particularly fond of window glazing, or your neighbour's business. In which case—bore away.

➤ CHOOSE YOUR WORDS WISELY

Avoid clichés and opt for colourful, descriptive, emotive language. Why say "my feelings are affected" when you could write "you pierce my soul"? Remember, things are not merely painful, they are *agony*, they are not understood, but *penetrate*, you are not just loyal, you are *fervent* and *undeviating*.

➤ ASK QUESTIONS

This creates the obligation of a reply, thus giving you another chance to send a letter, and the cycle continues.

A HEROINE WHO'S GOOD
AT KEEPING SECRETS

ELINOR DASHWOOD

"Sometimes one is guided by what they say of themselves, and very frequently by what other people say of them, without giving oneself time to deliberate and judge."

Sense and Sensibility, Chapter XVII

Give everyone a chance—make judgements based on their actions, rather than jumping into the pool of gossip (no matter how salacious the rumours from last month's ball with the regiment might be).

**EMMA WOODHOUSE'S
DISAPPROVING BROTHER-TYPE**

George Knightley

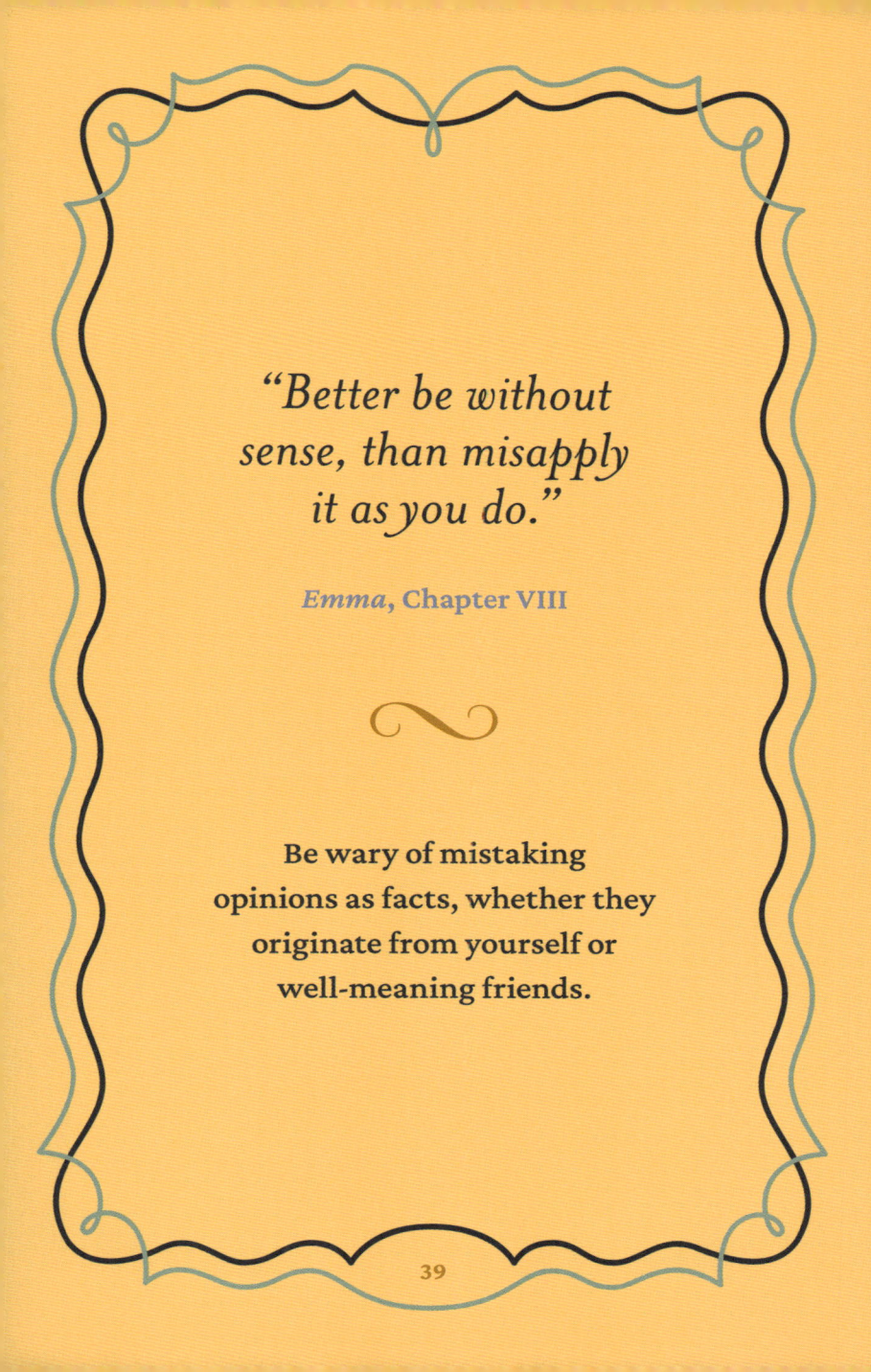

"Better be without sense, than misapply it as you do."

Emma, Chapter VIII

Be wary of mistaking opinions as facts, whether they originate from yourself or well-meaning friends.

ELIZABETH BENNET'S GOOD FRIEND

CHARLOTTE LUCAS

"We can all begin freely—a slight preference is natural enough; but there are very few of us who have heart enough to be really in love without encouragement."

Pride and Prejudice, Chapter VI

When it comes to love, communication must never be neglected (or obviously studied).

NARRATOR

NORTHANGER ABBEY

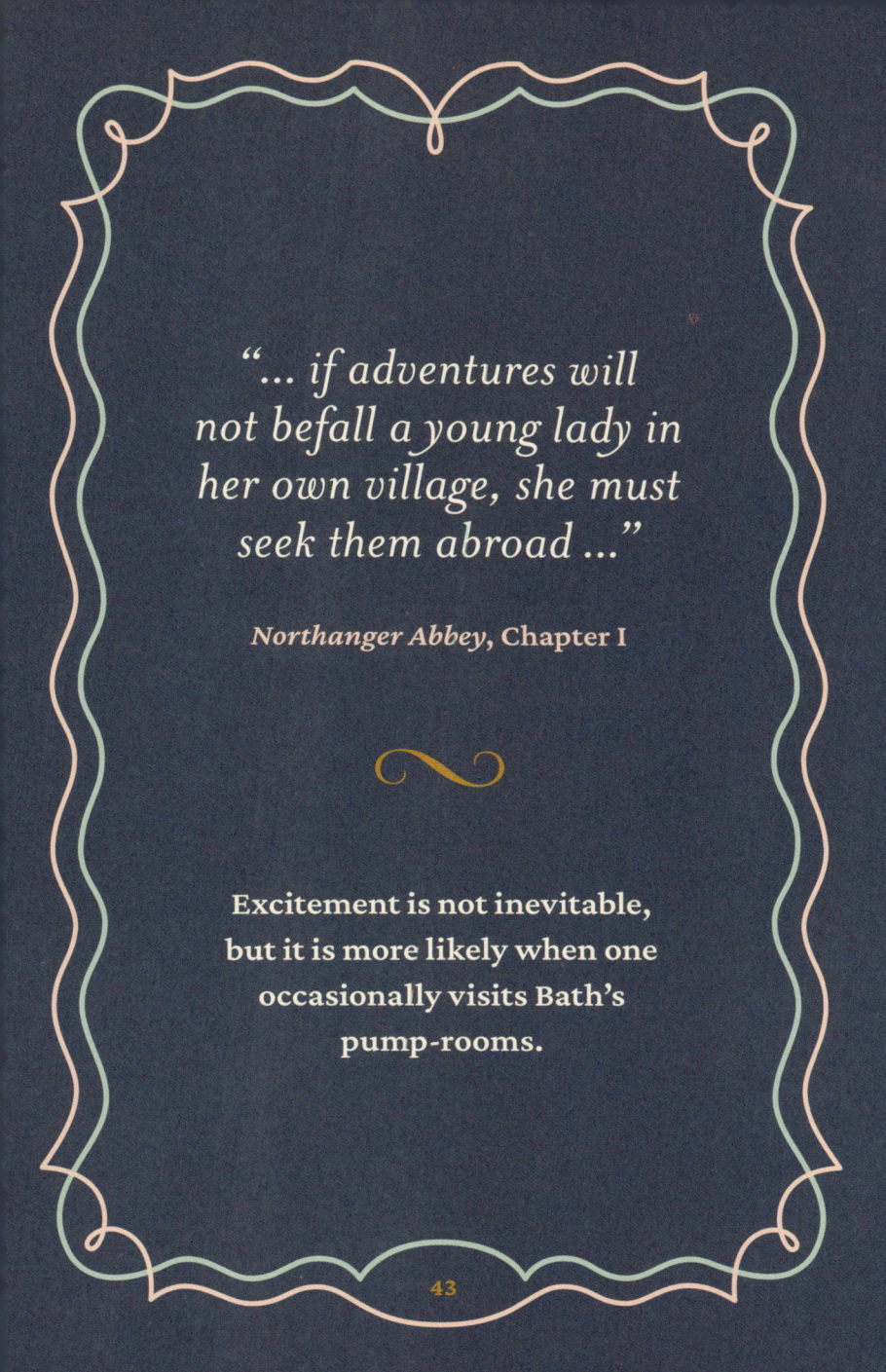

"... if adventures will not befall a young lady in her own village, she must seek them abroad ..."

Northanger Abbey, Chapter I

∞

Excitement is not inevitable, but it is more likely when one occasionally visits Bath's pump-rooms.

Convalescing After an Ill-Conceived Stroll in the Rain

A stroll for fresh air can leave you with just the opposite—confined to bed for a month, with nothing to do and no one to see, and certainly no new air to breathe. While you dirty your stockings walking in the fields, always heed the horizon, as being caught in the rain is a grave danger to one's health. However, if you have already made this mistake (or your mama forced you to visit a nearby bachelor by foot), here are some suggestions for passing the hours:

- See what interesting pictures your mind can form with the mould spots on the ceiling.
- Flick through your letter collection as swiftly as possible so that you absorb only one or two words from each sentence, overwhelming your already tired mind and allowing no space for a unique thought to enter.
- Ask the servants for the latest gossip. They know everything about everyone. Everything.
- Have your siblings act out scenes from your favourite book. If they truly love you, they'll perform for ten hours without pause.
- Draw a self-portrait, but try not to compare it to those done in healthier times. It will not end well for your self-esteem.
- Re-read your childhood diary and laugh at how ridiculous you were. Write letters to all your friends telling them about it. They will not care, but you shall enjoy it nonetheless.
- Eat.
- Eat more.
- If you happen to be convalescing at the object of your affection's abode (courtesy of your mother's machinations), avoid contact at all costs. It would not only be scandalous, but very bad for your prospects. Who wants to propose to someone after witnessing their bodily fluids oozing?
- Most importantly, rest. The sooner you are better, the sooner you can return to your regularly scheduled ennui.

ELINOR DASHWOOD'S MOTHER

MRS DASHWOOD

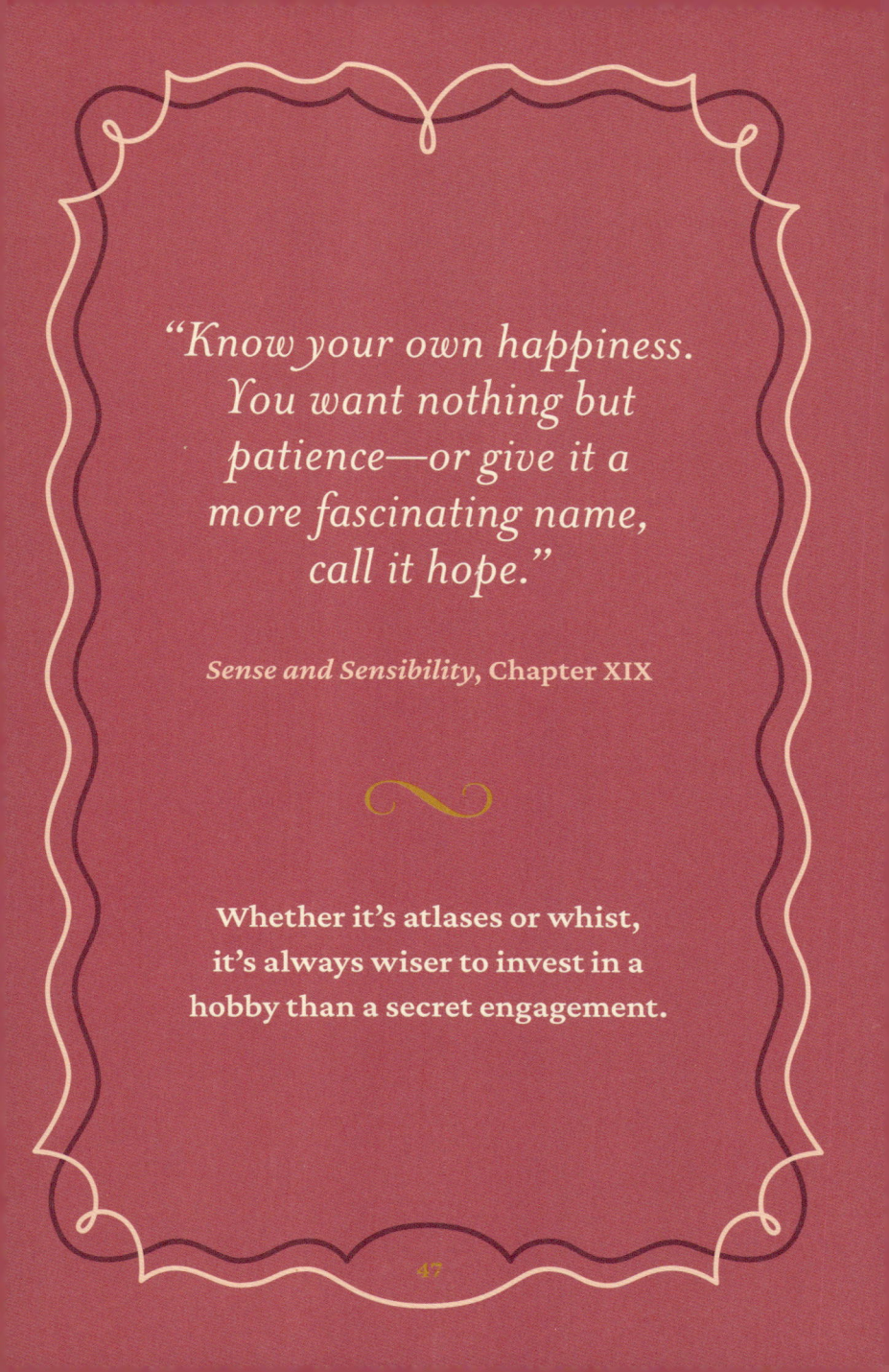

"Know your own happiness. You want nothing but patience—or give it a more fascinating name, call it hope."

Sense and Sensibility, Chapter XIX

Whether it's atlases or whist, it's always wiser to invest in a hobby than a secret engagement.

AN AVID DANCER AND FRIEND
OF EMMA WOODHOUSE

FRANK CHURCHILL

"—why not seize the pleasure at once?—How often is happiness destroyed by preparation, foolish preparation!"

Emma, Chapter XII

∞

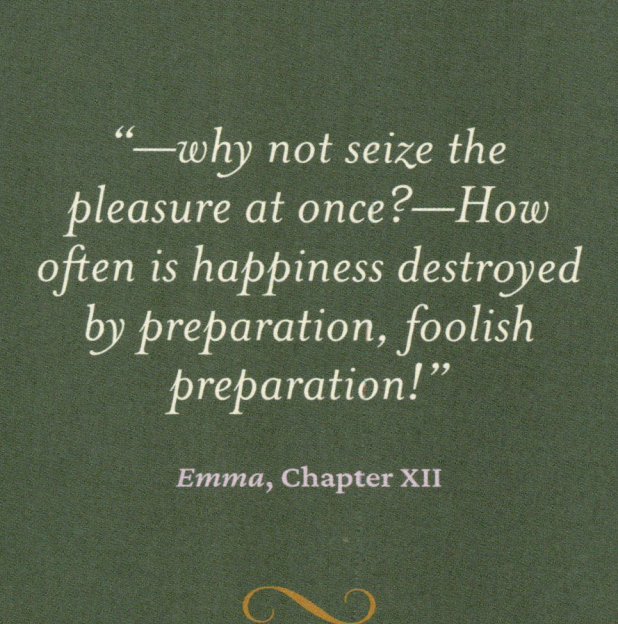

Prudence has its time and place, but waiting until the death of a family member for happiness is generally ill-advised.

THE MOST ELIGIBLE OF
AUSTEN'S BACHELORS

MR COLLINS

> "... though I sometimes amuse myself with suggesting and arranging such little elegant compliments as may be adapted to ordinary occasions, I always wish to give them as unstudied an air as possible."

Pride and Prejudice, Chapter XIV

Practice makes perfect, even when it comes to marriage proposals.

Embarrassing Things Your Family Does, Ranked

There is no one as dear as family, and no one more capable of inflicting embarrassment in public. No one will you love you as much and care as little when you explain how their actions have made you *wretched*. Here is an incomplete list of their many methods, from least to most mortifying:

10. SINGING LOUDLY AND FREQUENTLY

One too many public renditions of Handel's "Largo" is mortifying indeed.

9. WORKING IN TRADE

It is perfectly respectable to work, but it is far more respectable to not work at all.

8. FLIRTING WITH THE ENTIRE REGIMENT

Your siblings may be entitled to their fun ...

7. RUNNING AWAY WITH AN OFFICER

... but fun can go too far. Of course, the shame should lie with the officer, not your very young, very naïve family member. But society never sees it that way.

6. NAME-DROPPING

Yes, we KNOW you know Lady de Blah Blah, you do not need to mention it in every sentence. Or ever again.

5. APPROACHING OTHERS WITHOUT INTRODUCTION

This is even worse when combined with a name-drop.

4. BANISHING YOUR BELOVED

Nothing damages a prospective marriage more than a parent forcing your soon-to-be betrothed into the earliest possible carriage due to a misunderstanding.

3. DISMISSING A DEAD PARENT'S WISHES

Few individuals are crasser than a brother who ignores a father's wishes to look after his mother and sisters.

2. BRAG ABOUT AN ENGAGEMENT

It is understandable that your parents are excited about your good match. It is unbearable when they announce the marriage before anyone has asked for your hand.

1. OPENLY LOATHE YOUR GUESTS

When your mama has never heard of "forgiving and forgetting," it does make your enemies-to-lovers journey rather difficult.

ELINOR DASHWOOD'S
GENEROUS SISTER-IN-LAW

FANNY DASHWOOD

"... people always live for ever when there is any annuity to be paid them... An annuity is a very serious business; it comes over and over every year, and there is no getting rid of it."

***Sense and Sensibility*, Chapter II**

While generosity and charity of the spirit are well and good, you should never forget yourself while trying to take care of others—even when they are your in-laws.

CATHERINE MORLAND'S CRUSH
AND SOMETIMES TUTOR

Henry Tilney

"To be always firm must be to be often obstinate."

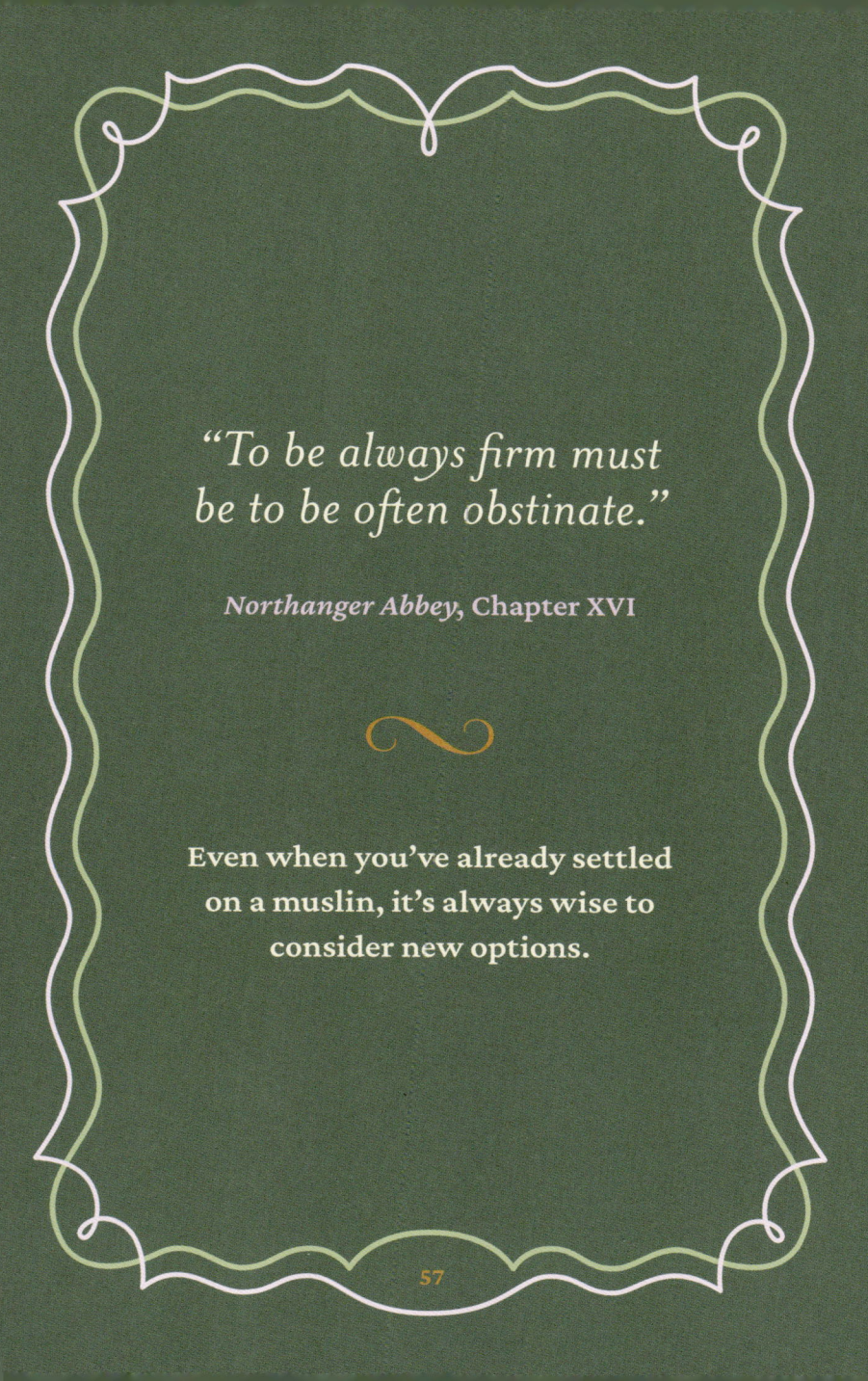

Northanger Abbey, Chapter XVI

～∞～

Even when you've already settled on a muslin, it's always wise to consider new options.

EMMA WOODHOUSE'S FORMER GOVERNESS AND CURRENT FRIEND

MRS WESTON

> "… do not pretend, with your sweet temper, to understand a bad one, or to lay down rules for it: you must let it go its own way."

Emma, Chapter XIV

It's a waste of energy trying to understand why others won't change.

An Introvert's Guide to Balls

~

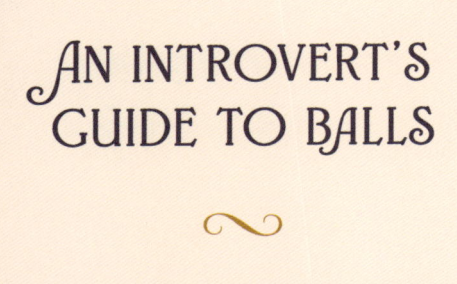

Balls are a delight to all—unless you are shy and retiring. In that case, they can be excessively wearying, even if you occasionally enjoy the Boulangere. For those of a reclusive temperament, here are ways to enhance your enjoyment, or at least expediate your recovery from the season's gatherings:

➤ HAVE A LARGE FORTUNE

Money matters more than anything—even the perceived rudeness that extends from your guarded feelings. If you cannot be polite, try at least to be rich.

➤ DESIGNATE A CHAMPION

Bring a close friend to come to your rescue when you are trapped by that one tiresome acquaintance of your cousin.

➤ WALK IN CIRCLES

This way, you will look excessively busy, and it will never be clear just how little you are engaging with anyone or anything.

➤ DANCE

Unfortunately, it simply must be done at least once or twice, for appearance's sake. Warm up with a strong tea, or whatever your tipple of choice may be.

➤ HAVE AN EXCUSE TO LEAVE

Prepare one ahead of time so that you are ready to escape. If possible, have a servant extricate you. Ensure the excuse is strong enough—a death in the family should suffice.

➤ GLARE FROM THE CORNER AS THOUGH YOU ARE SUPERIOR TO EVERYONE ELSE

Actually, this is a jest. Never, under any circumstances, do this. And especially never voice your superiority out loud. Even if there is no one nearby who is handsome enough to tempt you, keep that to yourself, for heaven's sake.

➤ GO HOME AND CRY

You have worked hard. You deserve it.

A MISTREATED HEROINE

FANNY PRICE

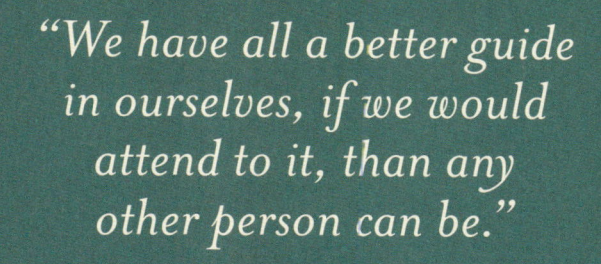

"We have all a better guide in ourselves, if we would attend to it, than any other person can be."

Mansfield Park, Chapter XLII

While your suitor may be rich and dashing, it's always better to listen to your gut than take advice from your relatives.

NARRATOR

Sense and Sensibility

"She was stronger alone, and her own good sense so well supported her, that her firmness was as unshaken, her appearance of cheerfulness as invariable, as with regrets so poignant and so fresh, it was possible for them to be."

Sense and Sensibility, Chapter XXIII

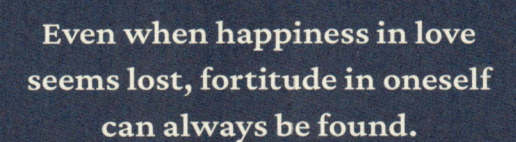

Even when happiness in love seems lost, fortitude in oneself can always be found.

EMMA WOODHOUSE'S FATHER AND WARD

MR WOODHOUSE

"I never had much opinion of the sea air."

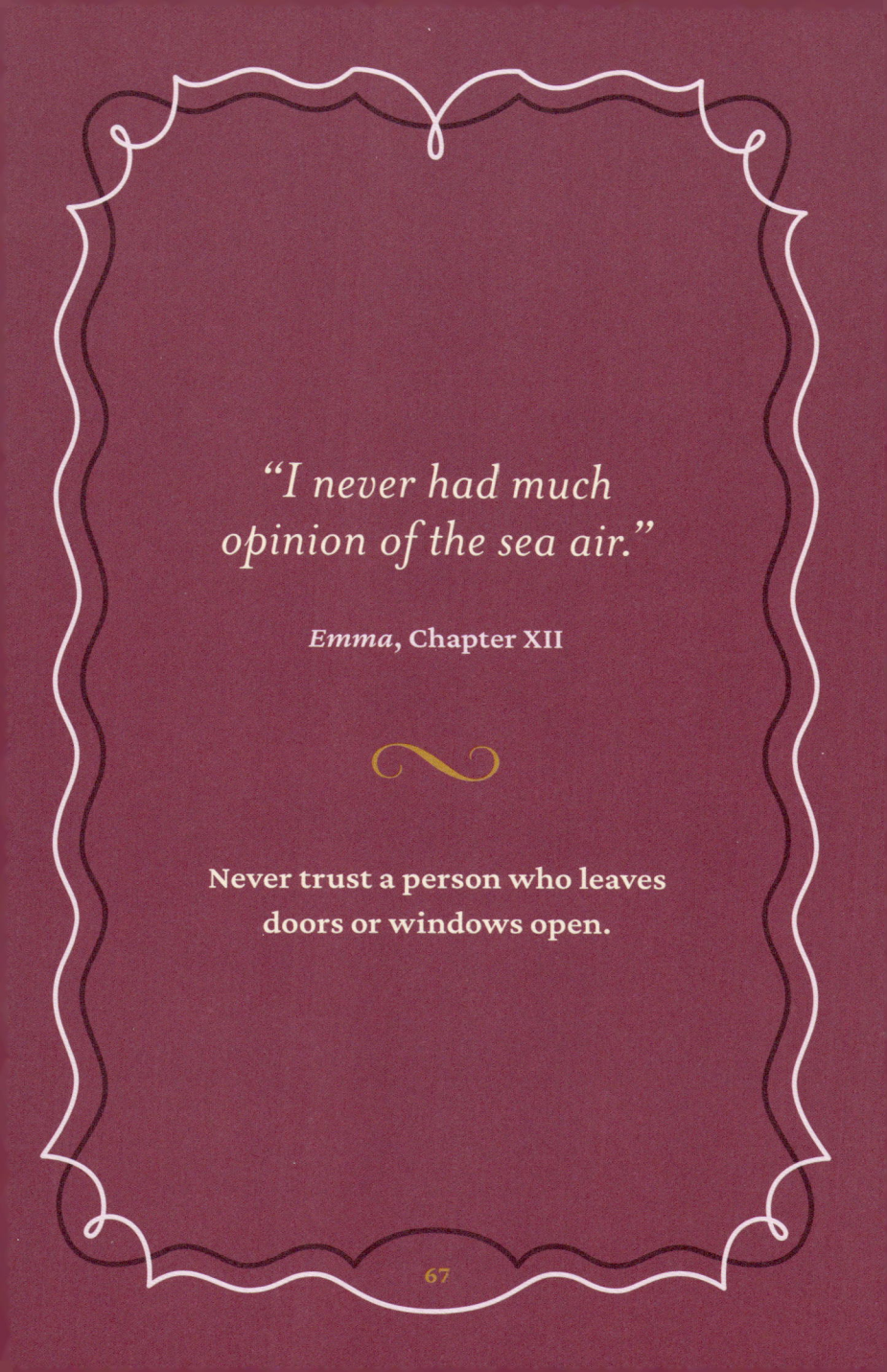

Emma, Chapter XII

∾

Never trust a person who leaves doors or windows open.

A SUFFERER OF NERVES

Mrs Bennet

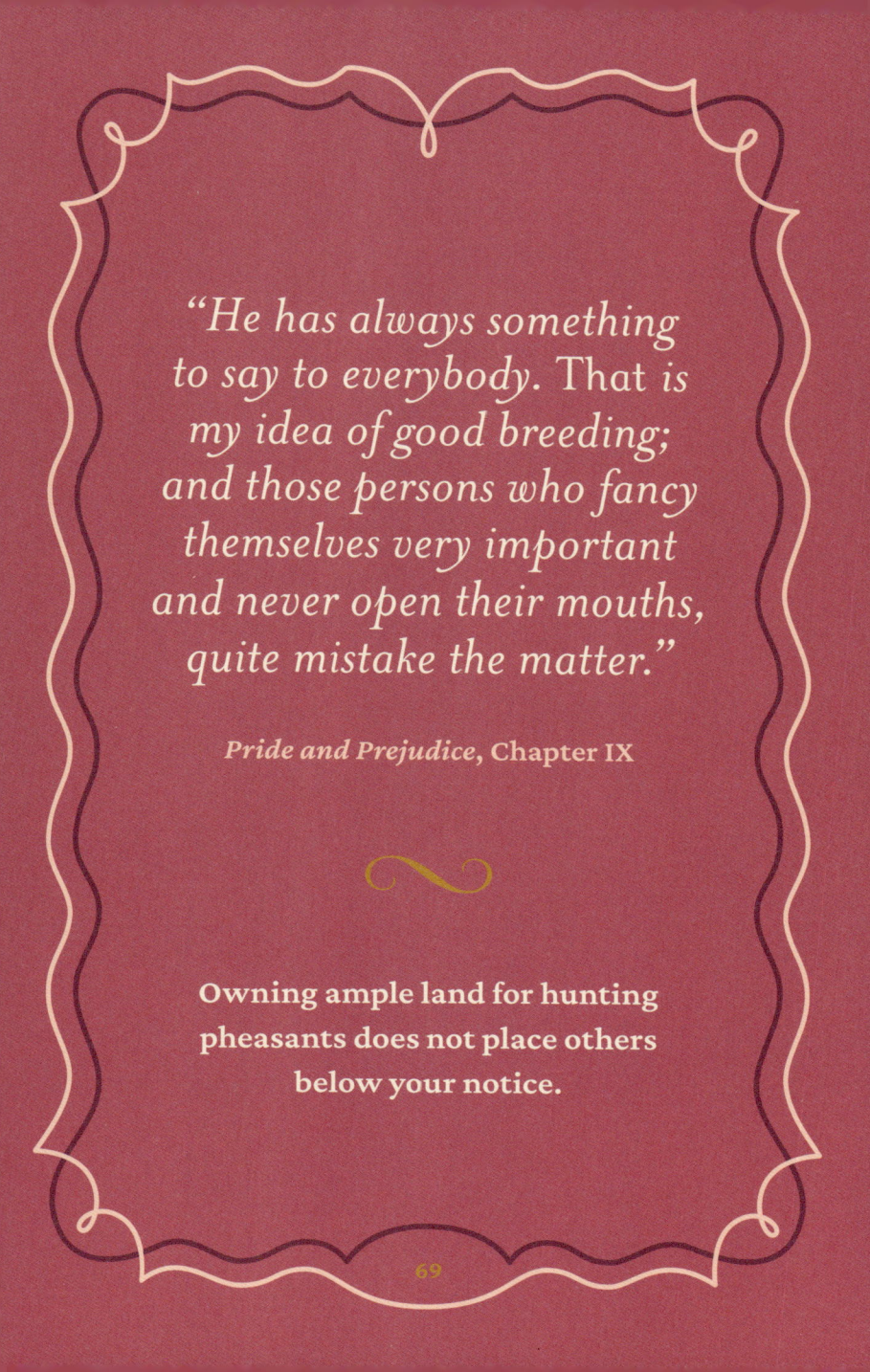

"He has always something to say to everybody. That is my idea of good breeding; and those persons who fancy themselves very important and never open their mouths, quite mistake the matter."

Pride and Prejudice, **Chapter IX**

Owning ample land for hunting pheasants does not place others below your notice.

What to Do When You Are This Week's Gossip

~

Have you recently had a secret engagement revealed? Gambled away most of your inheritance in London? Committed a faux pas at an ill-conceived picnic? Whatever improprieties you have committed, you may find solace in these acts:

- Crying.

- Laughing.

- Laughing and crying at the same time.

- Hiding in your room while you simultaneously laugh and cry.

- Thinking long and hard about every mistake you have ever made in an hours-long spiral of agonising self-reflection, self-blame, and self-hatred.

- Standing outside and raging at the universe. Dig a hole and scream into it. Direct your anger at everyone but yourself. Get drenched. Become sick. Develop a fever so severe you scare everyone into forgetting anything but their sympathies.

- Taking comfort in your sincere friends. They are the ones who will remain by your side.

- Unless they are the ones you wronged. If you are truly in the wrong: apologise. If you are not truly in the wrong but still want to have a social life: apologise.

- Starting a rumour about someone else. Preferably one of your neighbours who is gossiping about you. Ensure this rumour cannot be traced back to you, or you may be the subject of gossip all over again.

- If all else fails, accept your cousin's proposal and accept a life several counties away. Anything is better than being discussed in drawing rooms for the rest of the season, unless that is your goal. In which case, bask in the obvious glances.

ANNE ELLIOT'S SCHOOL FRIEND

MRS SMITH

"... she has a fund of good sense and observation, which ... make her infinitely superior to thousands of those who having only received 'the best education in the world,' know nothing worth attending to."

Persuasion, Chapter XVII

There is more to life than mastering the modern languages and designing tables.

A HEROINE WITH AN
OVERACTIVE IMAGINATION

CATHERINE MORLAND

"*If I am wrong, I am doing what I believe to be right.*"

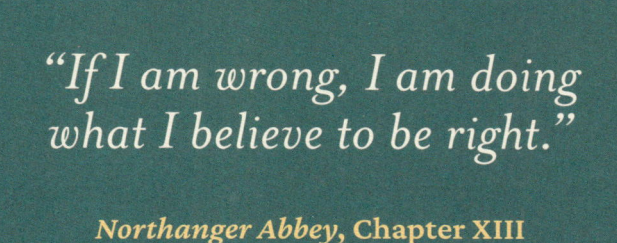

Northanger Abbey, **Chapter XIII**

No matter how tempting a friend's scheme may sound, no trip to an old castle is worth breaking a promise to another.

ANNE ELLIOT'S BROTHER-IN-LAW

CHARLES MUSGROVE

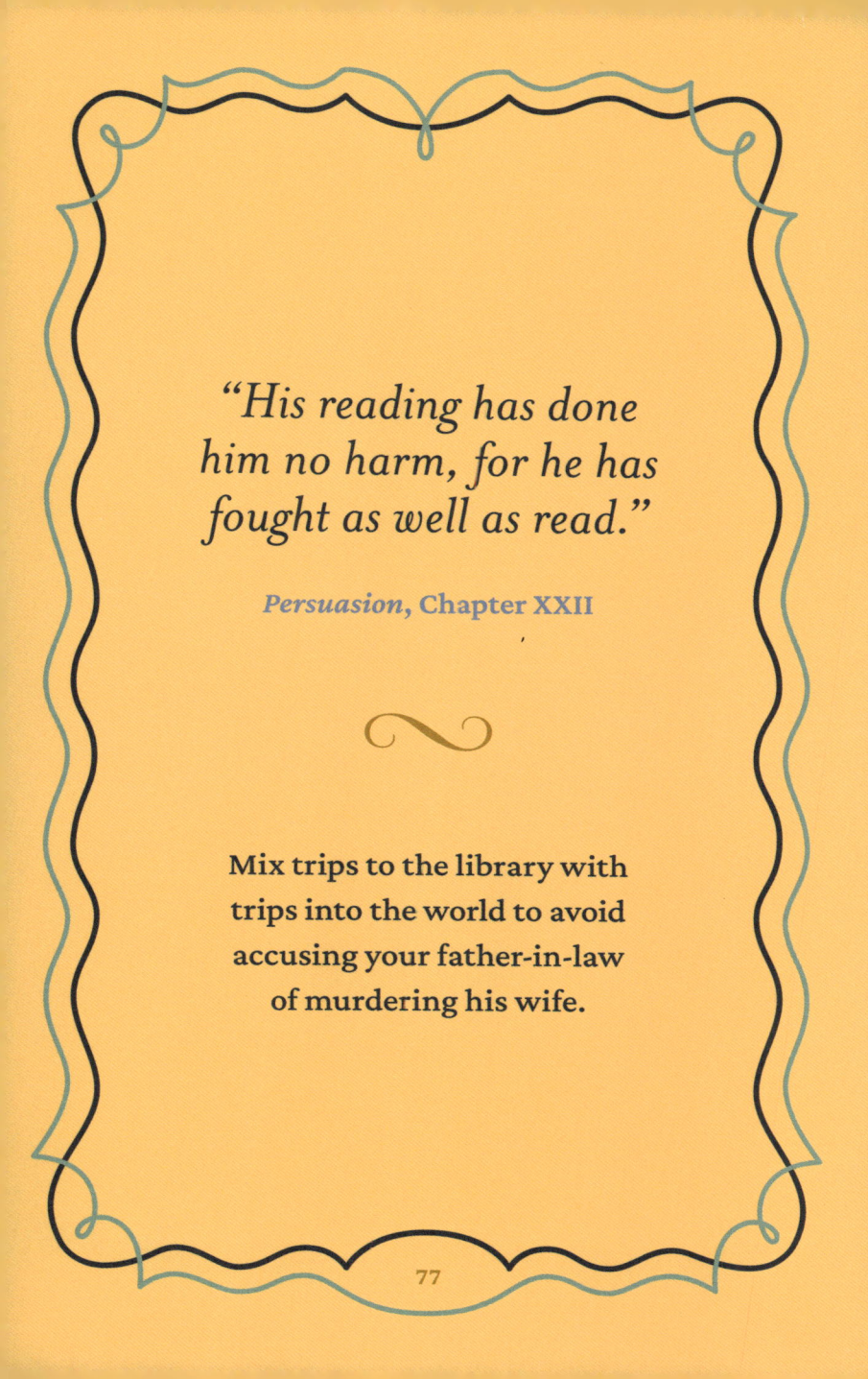

"His reading has done him no harm, for he has fought as well as read."

***Persuasion*, Chapter XXII**

∾

Mix trips to the library with trips into the world to avoid accusing your father-in-law of murdering his wife.

What to Consider Before Saying "Yes"

While it may seem judicious to immediately accept an offer of marriage, it is always wise to listen to oneself, rather than any mothers/uncles/aunts/aristocratic relatives of your love interest. When in doubt, consider:

THEIR FORTUNE

If marriage isn't for love, it should at least be for extensive, well-tended gardens.

THEIR PROXIMITY TO YOUR PARENTS

Too close, and you will see your parents far too often. Too far, and they will visit for far too long.

THEIR PAST

Are there any previous broken engagements you should be concerned about? Or worse—*unbroken* engagements?

THEIR OCCUPATION

Your betrothed's occupation is as good as yours. Do you want a life of adventure—and risk—with a soldier? To be sermonised in your own home by a vicar? To be forced to wade through muck with a farmer? Or to do virtually nothing with a gentleman?

THEIR APPEARANCE

While a handsome visage will fade with time, you want to at least tolerate your spouse's looks for the foreseeable future.

THEIR ABILITY TO CONVERSE AND DANCE

For better or worse, they will be your primary conversation and dancing partner for life, so make sure they can avoid stepping on toes.

THEIR HEALTH

Do you want a long future with them? Or would you prefer to keep it short? The state of their health is particularly pertinent, no matter which way you answer.

THEIR AGE *See above.*

YOUR AGE

Do you have time to find a better match? (The correct answer is always yes, despite what relatives may say.)

WHETHER YOU LOVE THEM

Not a must, but a nice bonus.

THE BEST-READ OF THE BENNET SISTERS

MARY BENNET

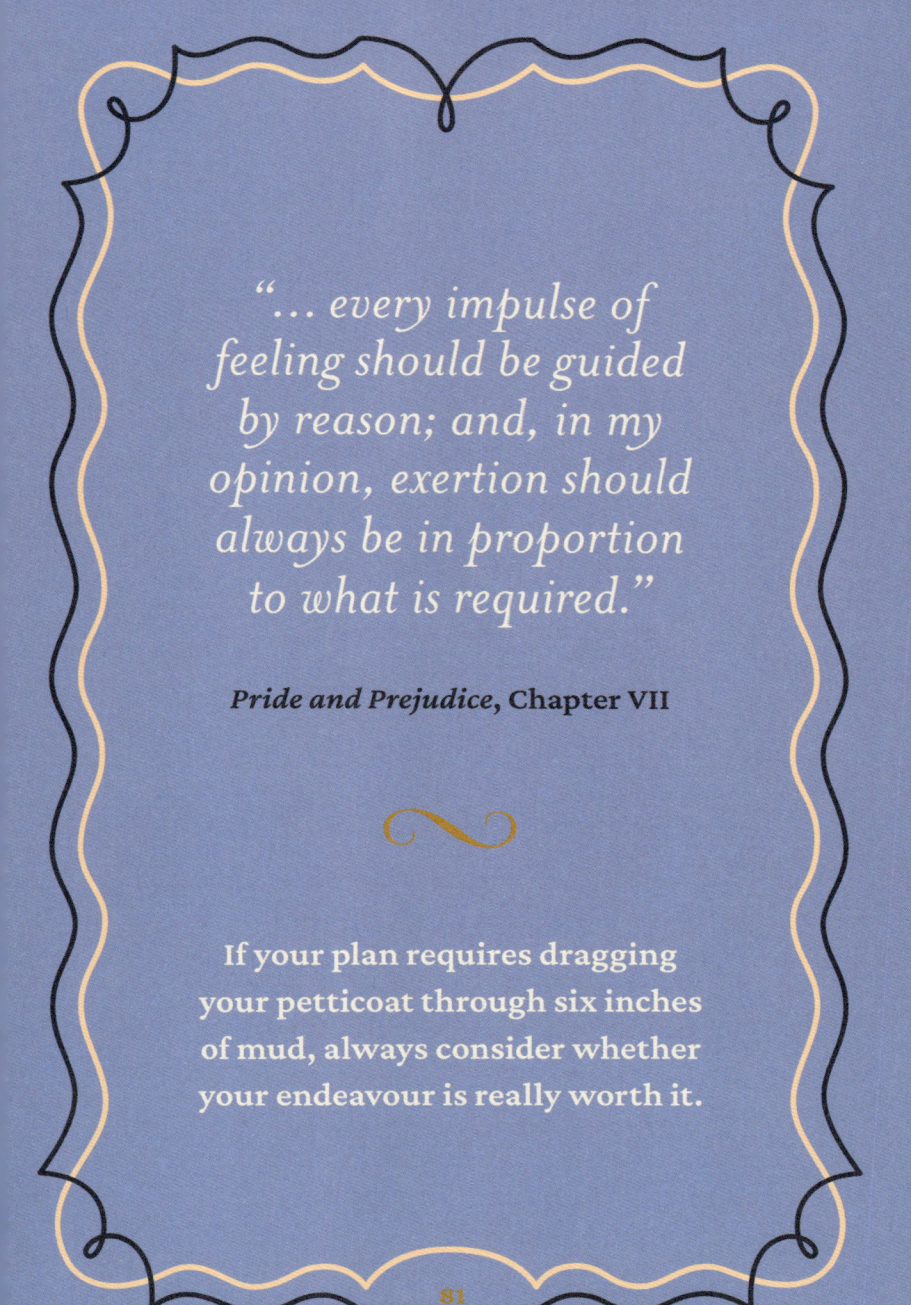

"... every impulse of feeling should be guided by reason; and, in my opinion, exertion should always be in proportion to what is required."

Pride and Prejudice, **Chapter VII**

If your plan requires dragging your petticoat through six inches of mud, always consider whether your endeavour is really worth it.

NARRATOR

MANSFIELD PARK

"There is nothing like employment, active indispensable employment, for relieving sorrow. Employment, even melancholy, may dispel melancholy …"

Mansfield Park, Chapter XLVI

If a friend's sudden marriage to a clergy member has left you bereft, there's no better time to finally clean the house.

A MAN WITH TOO MUCH TIME
AND CHARM ON HIS HANDS

Henry Crawford

"It is he who sees and worships your merit the strongest, who loves you most devotedly, that has the best right to a return."

Mansfield Park, **Chapter XXXIV**

We all deserve love that goes deeper than empty words and an affair with our cousin.

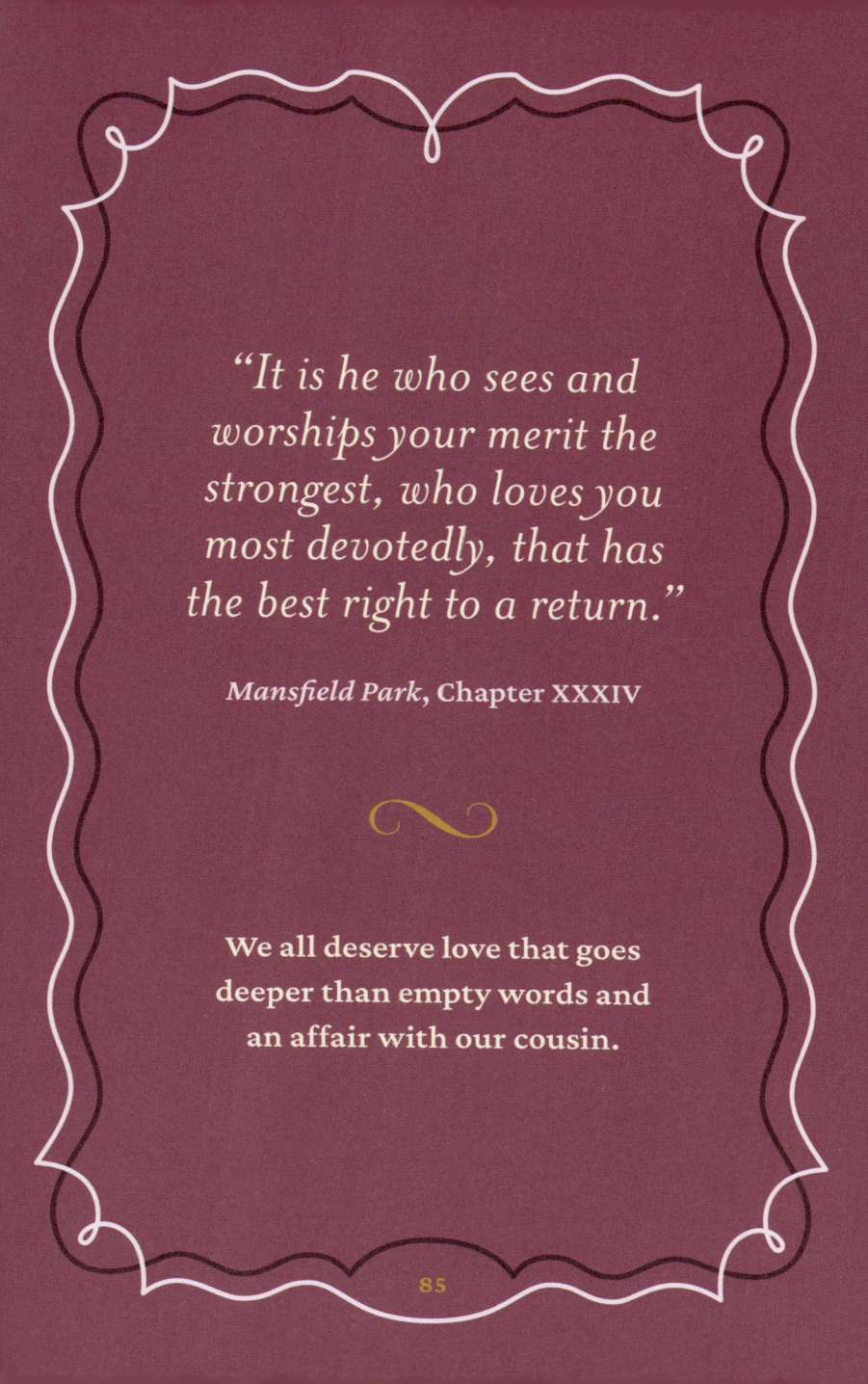

SIGNS HE'S A RAKE YOU (AND YOUR SISTERS) SHOULD AVOID

A quick smile and a quicker wit can prove hard to resist—particularly when no new families have joined the neighbourhood for several seasons. Caution, however, will never go amiss if a strapping figure appears right as you've twisted an ankle. Red flags that are prudent to heed:

➤ HE IS A PRODIGIOUS FLIRT

He may be an agreeable companion, but there is such a thing as *too* agreeable. Especially when it involves literally every acquaintance he meets.

➤ HE HAS *TOO* EXCELLENT A HEAD OF HAIR

Have you never seen such a full bouffant? Do his sideburns cover at least 67 per cent of his cheeks? These are clear indications he takes far too much care of his appearance, and not enough of other people.

➤ HE LOVES TO TALK

He volunteers information without you prying it out of him. Very suspicious and unnatural indeed.

➤ HE HOLDS HIMSELF IN HIGH ESTEEM

A small amount of confidence is healthy and becoming, but not if he chooses himself above all others—and especially you.

➤ HE CARRIES HIS SELF-PORTRAIT

Unsolicited portrait displays can be very troubling and tedious.

➤ HE BREAKS ENGAGEMENTS

Whether it's a social engagement or a promise of marriage, if he breaks it, he is nothing but a profligate rake.

➤ HE WEARS A RED COAT

He may look dashing, but he is merely passing through your village. A literal walking red flag.

➤ HE DISAPPEARS WITHOUT A TRACE

Preferably, he does this without one of your sisters in tow.

A SHOCKINGLY OLD HEROINE

Anne Elliot

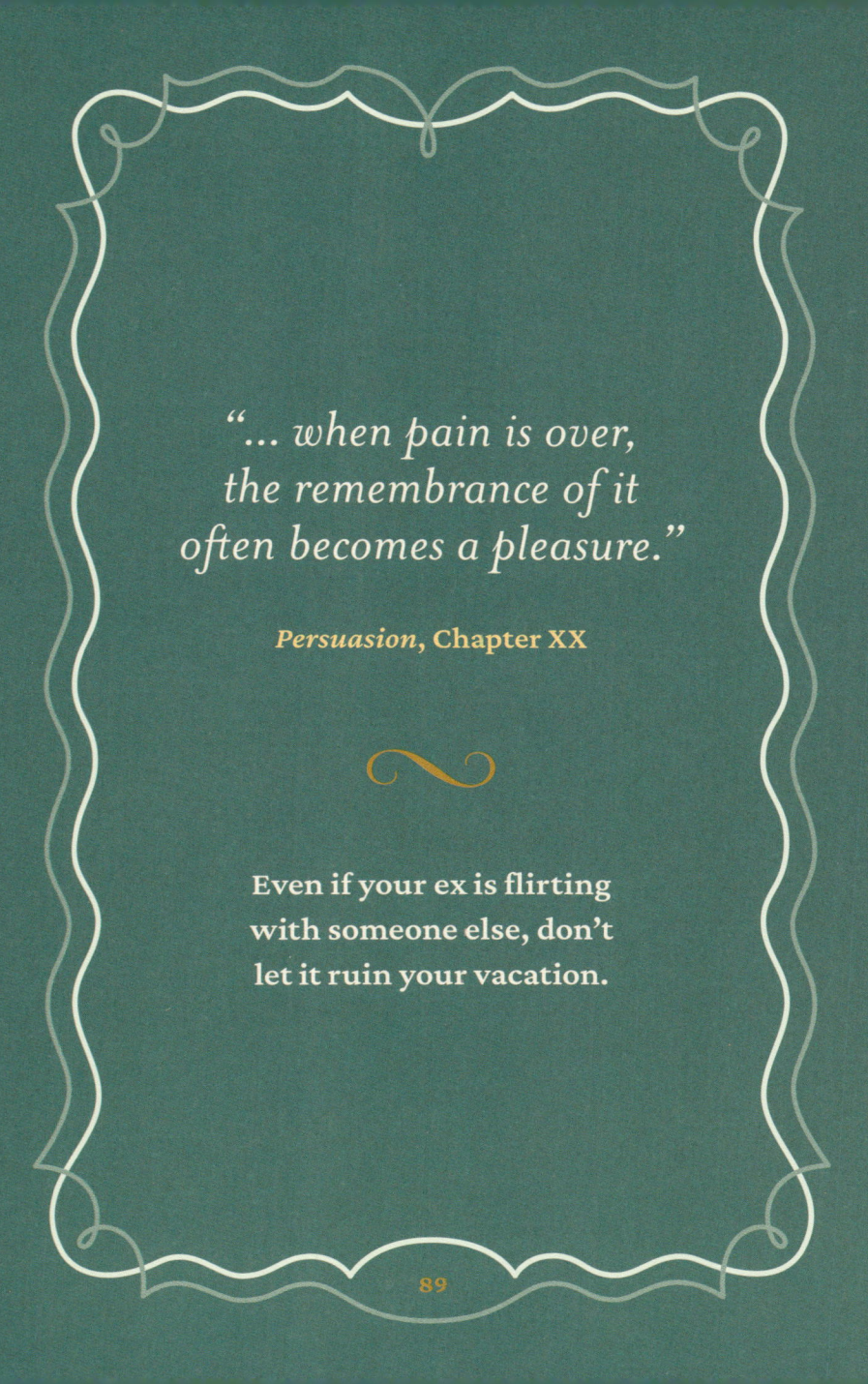

"... when pain is over, the remembrance of it often becomes a pleasure."

Persuasion, Chapter XX

Even if your ex is flirting with someone else, don't let it ruin your vacation.

FANNY PRICE'S COUSIN
AND LONG-TIME CRUSH

EDMUND BERTRAM

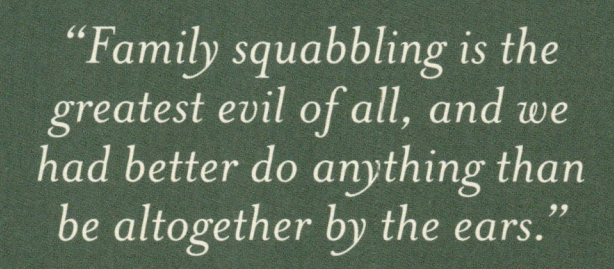

"Family squabbling is the greatest evil of all, and we had better do anything than be altogether by the ears."

Mansfield Park, Chapter XIII

∞

Not all battles are worth winning—sometimes, the play must go on.

CATHERINE MORLAND'S MOTHER

Mrs Morland

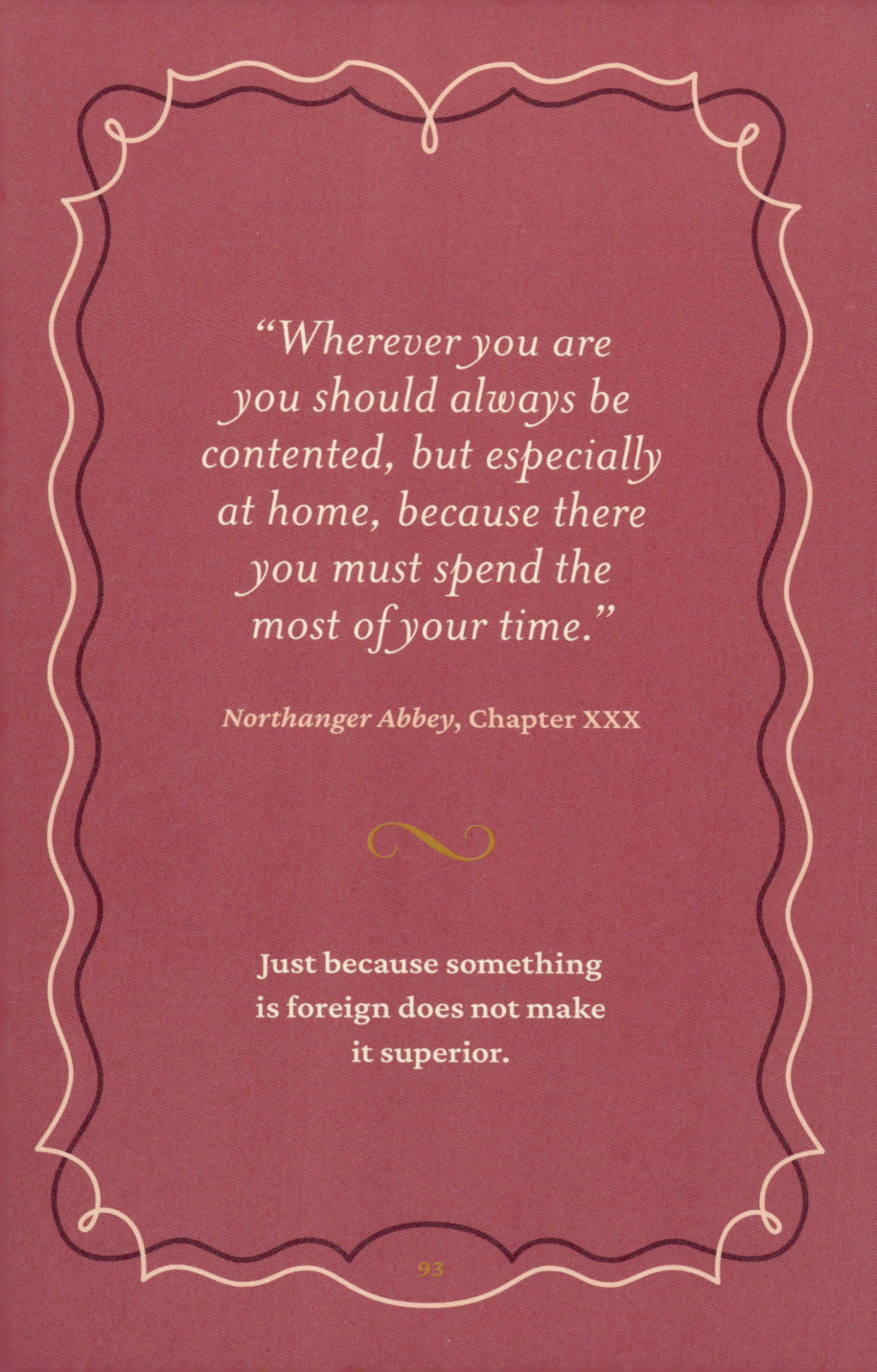

"Wherever you are you should always be contented, but especially at home, because there you must spend the most of your time."

Northanger Abbey, **Chapter XXX**

Just because something is foreign does not make it superior.

FRANK CHURCHILL'S FATHER

MR WESTON

> "What is right to be done cannot be done too soon."

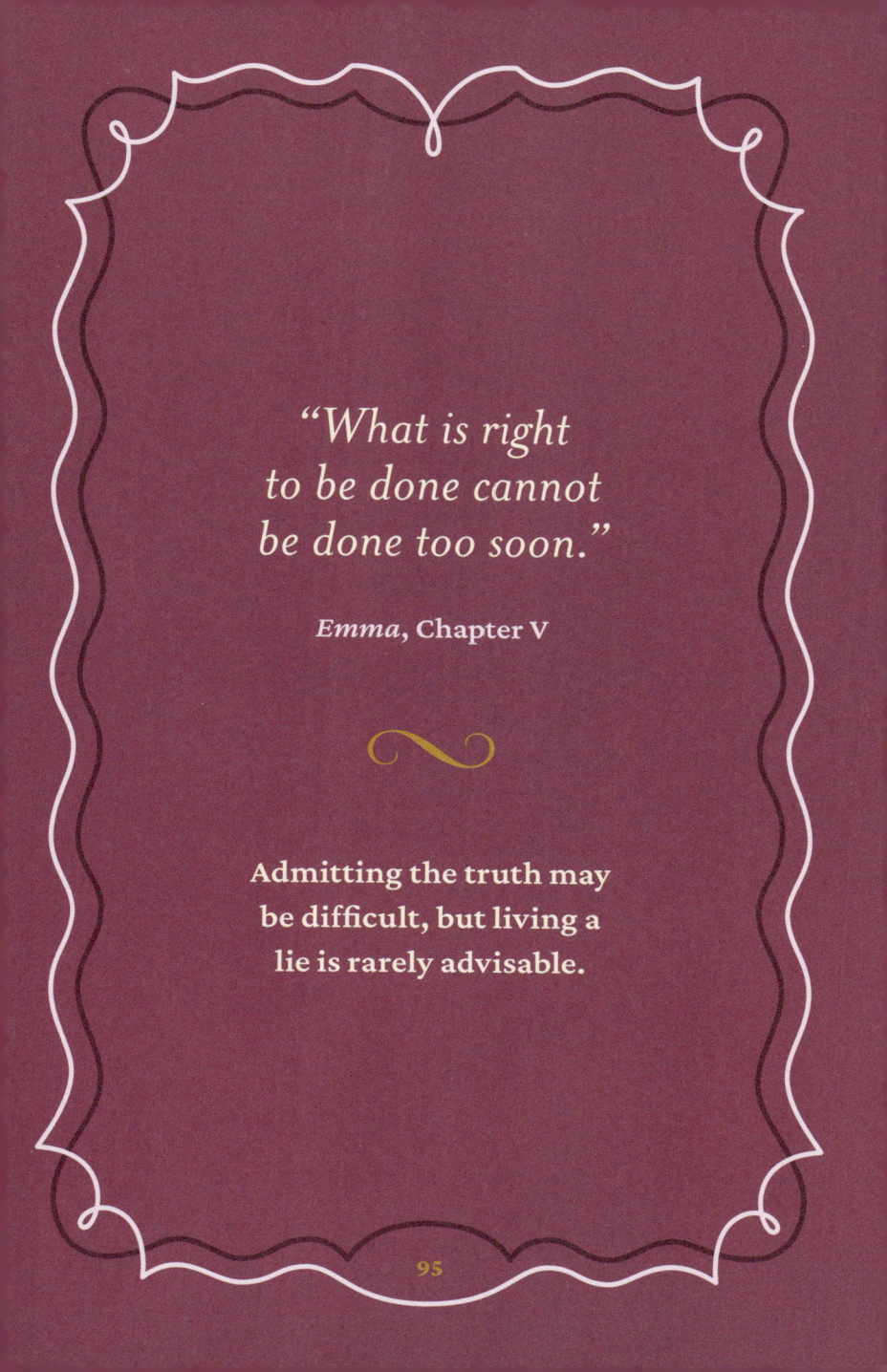

Emma, Chapter V

Admitting the truth may be difficult, but living a lie is rarely advisable.

THINGS ONLY TRUE FRIENDS UNDERSTAND

Your dearest friends: only they know the meanings of the many looks you pass at balls, conveying everything from "this person is most vexing" and "what a fine gentleman" to "we have much to discuss" and, most importantly, "get me out of here." True friends are the ones who know:

- 🪷 How to tighten your stays just enough that your figure looks flattering, but you can still breathe.

- 🪷 That you may have mistakenly talked them out of accepting a proposal from their long-time object of affection, but it was with the best of intentions.

- 🪷 To always walk on your left, as your right-hand profile is your most flattering.

- 🪷 How many glasses of punch you can have before your cheeks go red from the alcohol rather than the pinching.

- 🪷 To always arrange for you to stay with them when their wealthy cousin happens to be visiting from out of town.

- 🪷 To never applaud for your rival's piano performances too loudly.

- 🪷 That your company is worth keeping, despite your failures as a whist partner.

A MAN TO AVOID

JOHN WILLOUGHBY

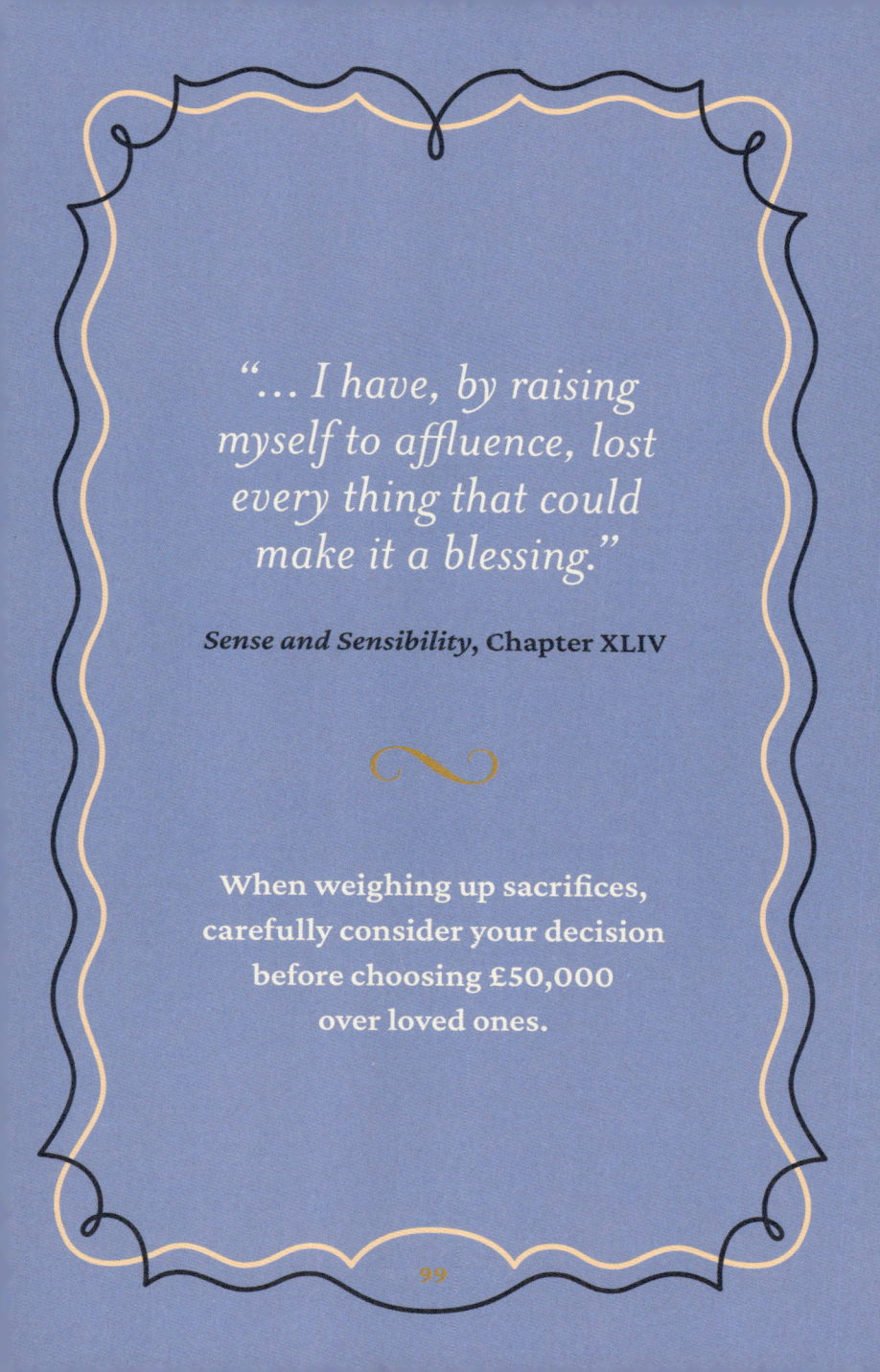

> "... I have, by raising myself to affluence, lost every thing that could make it a blessing."

***Sense and Sensibility*, Chapter XLIV**

When weighing up sacrifices, carefully consider your decision before choosing £50,000 over loved ones.

EMMA WOODHOUSE'S FRIEND
AND SOMETIMES VICTIM

HARRIET SMITH

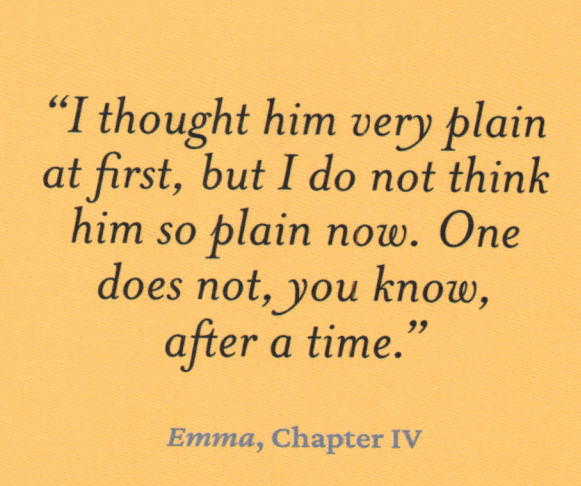

"I thought him very plain at first, but I do not think him so plain now. One does not, you know, after a time."

Emma, Chapter IV

There's nothing that improves one's appearance more than a fine character.

A MAN WHO'S RICH IN WEALTH
AND AWKWARDNESS

FITZWILLIAM DARCY

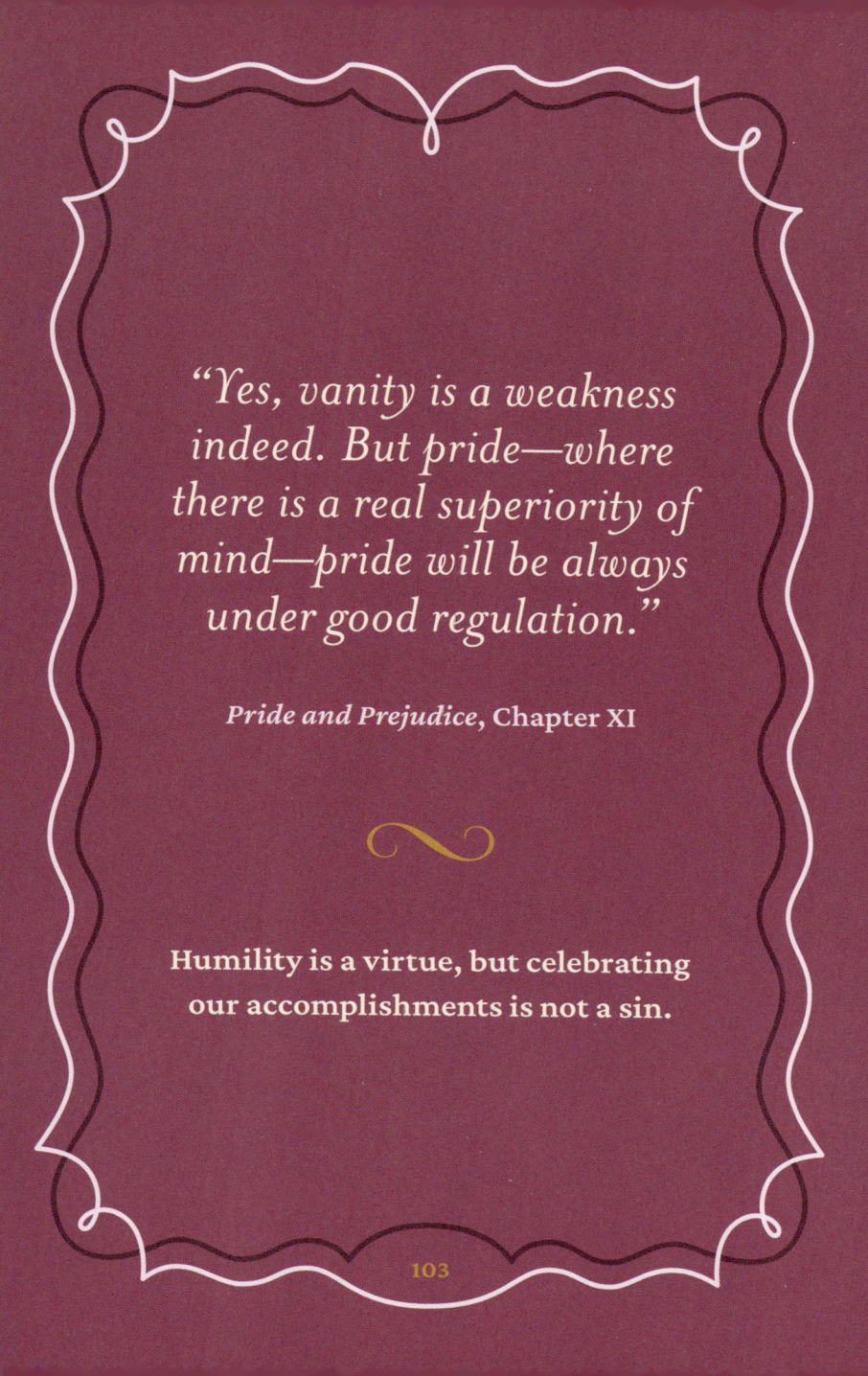

"Yes, vanity is a weakness indeed. But pride—where there is a real superiority of mind—pride will be always under good regulation."

Pride and Prejudice, **Chapter XI**

Humility is a virtue, but celebrating our accomplishments is not a sin.

Types of Acquaintances Every Circle Must Have

(even if you don't want them)

While we may shape our fates, we cannot shape our social circles. Circumstance and propriety require us to share pleasantries with neighbours who will, given the chance, invite themselves to pick strawberries on others' properties. You may move estates, but you will inevitably rediscover this same collection of figures:

THE WIT

Someone who loves a laugh and is quick enough to always find a reason for one. They are someone of keen intelligence, at least a mediocre education, and general good humour. At times, they may be a little too cutting, and insult, for instance, old and poor neighbours. In this case, they need to be reeled in by The Bore.

THE GOSSIP

They always know everyone else's business. This can become extremely tiresome when the business is yours, but it is also rather useful, not to mention entertaining. Gossip is a universal currency, after all.

THE CONFIDANTE

The calm friend and reliable listener who can keep a secret and shoulder all one's burdens. They are the natural enemy of The Gossip.

THE MATCHMAKER

Sometimes they are also The Gossip. They think they know better than everyone else, particularly when it comes to matters of the heart. Usually, they do not.

THE TROUBLEMAKER

A rebellious spirit who flouts conventions and paves their own way. Typically headstrong. A convenient acquaintance when one needs a distraction from one's own troubles—or, more importantly, when one needs The Gossip to be distracted.

THE ORGANISER

They may be irksome and overbearing, but without this person, who will organise trips to Box Hill?

THE OBLIGATION

This is not someone you—or anyone, really—want to spend time with, but you do not have a choice. It is a good thing their presence allows you to feel how truly generous and virtuous you are.

THE BORE

The wise, usually older friend who occasionally ruins all the fun by reminding everyone to be "good" and "kind" and "have manners." You are probably a little bit in love with them, even if you do not know it yet.

NARRATOR

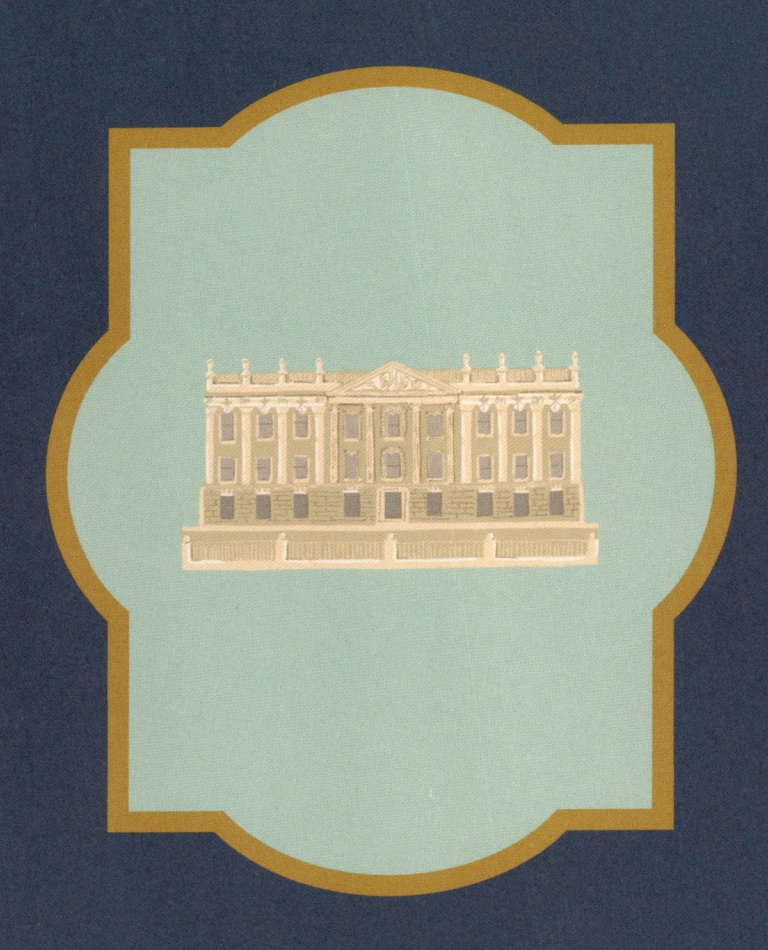

PRIDE AND PREJUDICE

"But how little of permanent happiness could belong to a couple who were only brought together because their passions were stronger than their virtue…"

Pride and Prejudice, Chapter L

∾

If your favourite things about your suitor are their striking features, it's probably not meant to be.

THE CRAWFORDS' SISTER

MRS
GRANT

"There will be little rubs and disappointments everywhere, and we are all apt to expect too much; but then, if one scheme of happiness fails, human nature turns to another; if the first calculation is wrong, we make a second better."

Mansfield Park, Chapter V

Failures of judgement are chances to create truer happiness (and to warn your sisters).

ELIZABETH BENNET'S
UNCLE FROM CHEAPSIDE

Mr Gardiner

> "Do not give way to useless alarm ... though it is right to be prepared for the worst, there is no occasion to look on it as certain."

Pride and Prejudice, Chapter XLVII

Even if your sister is dating your ex, don't assume all is lost.

Unexpected Places to Secure a Suitor

~

The ballroom is the natural setting for any budding match. But to truly secure your future—and, of course, love—you may have to gaze beyond the quadrille. It is best to never let your guard down when entering places such as:

◆ A HISTORICAL BUILDING

Whether it be a castle or an abbey, abandoned or lived in, these locations are fertile ground for romance. Something about the way they smell of dust and decay reminds us that life is fleeting and we must seize the day (and whoever happens to be standing in proximity).

◆ THE SICKBED

Unsightly rashes or putrid fluids should be kept to the privacy of one's home. But, say you have fallen off a seawall—well, then, there is no better place to be semi-conscious for days on end than in proximity to the person you plan to marry. It even affords you an easy way to assess their suitability: if they tend to you with care and skill, they are certainly deserving of your wit once you've recovered it.

◆ YOUR SUITOR'S OWN HOME

Showing up unannounced at the object of your desire's estate is a guaranteed way to gain their attention. Trust that they will delight in showing off their portrait collection and their many rooms in which one can take a turn in. They hopefully will not even find it odd or disturbing that you have arrived uninvited—it helps when they live in estates open to the public.

◆ YOUR OWN HOME

You may wonder how one could possibly find a match in the home. The only people there are servants and siblings and cousins! And it is true, two of those groups are completely inappropriate places to seek a marriage.

A LOVER OF PUGS AND
FANNY PRICE'S AUNT

Lady Bertram

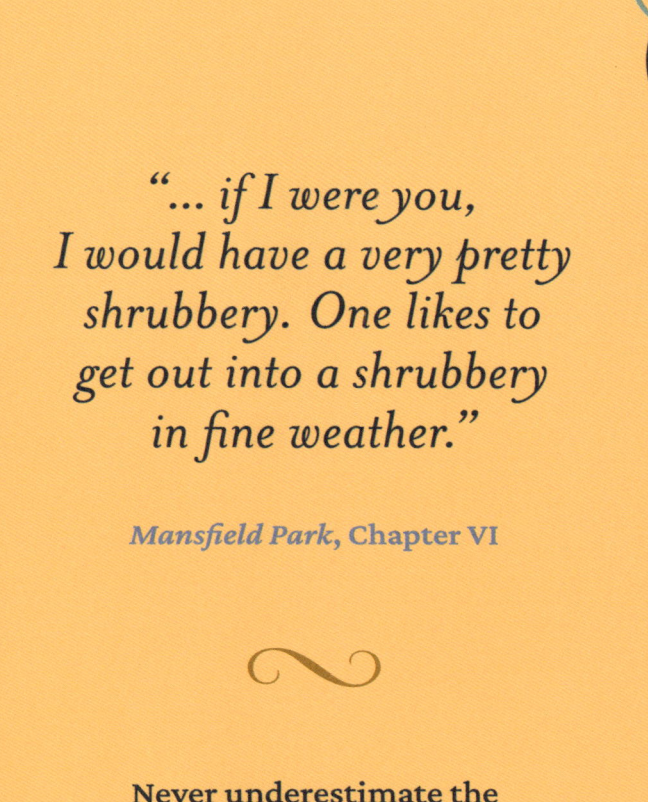

"... if I were you, I would have a very pretty shrubbery. One likes to get out into a shrubbery in fine weather."

Mansfield Park, Chapter VI

Never underestimate the improvements good hedges can make to your life.

DARCY'S FRIEND AND SOMETIMES VICTIM

CHARLES BINGLEY

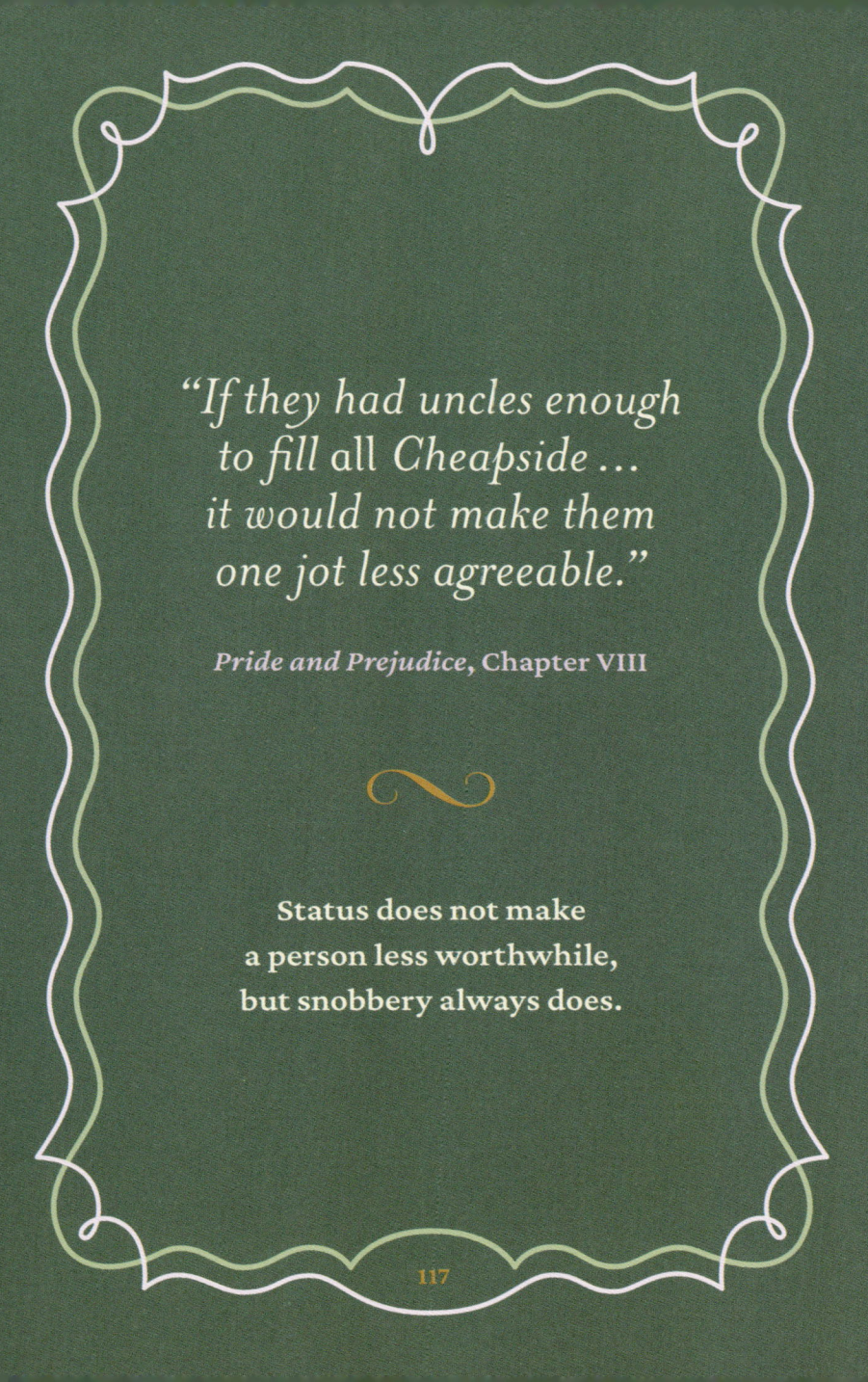

"If they had uncles enough to fill all Cheapside ... it would not make them one jot less agreeable."

Pride and Prejudice, Chapter VIII

Status does not make a person less worthwhile, but snobbery always does.

MR ELTON'S UNDERSTATED BRIDE

MRS ELTON

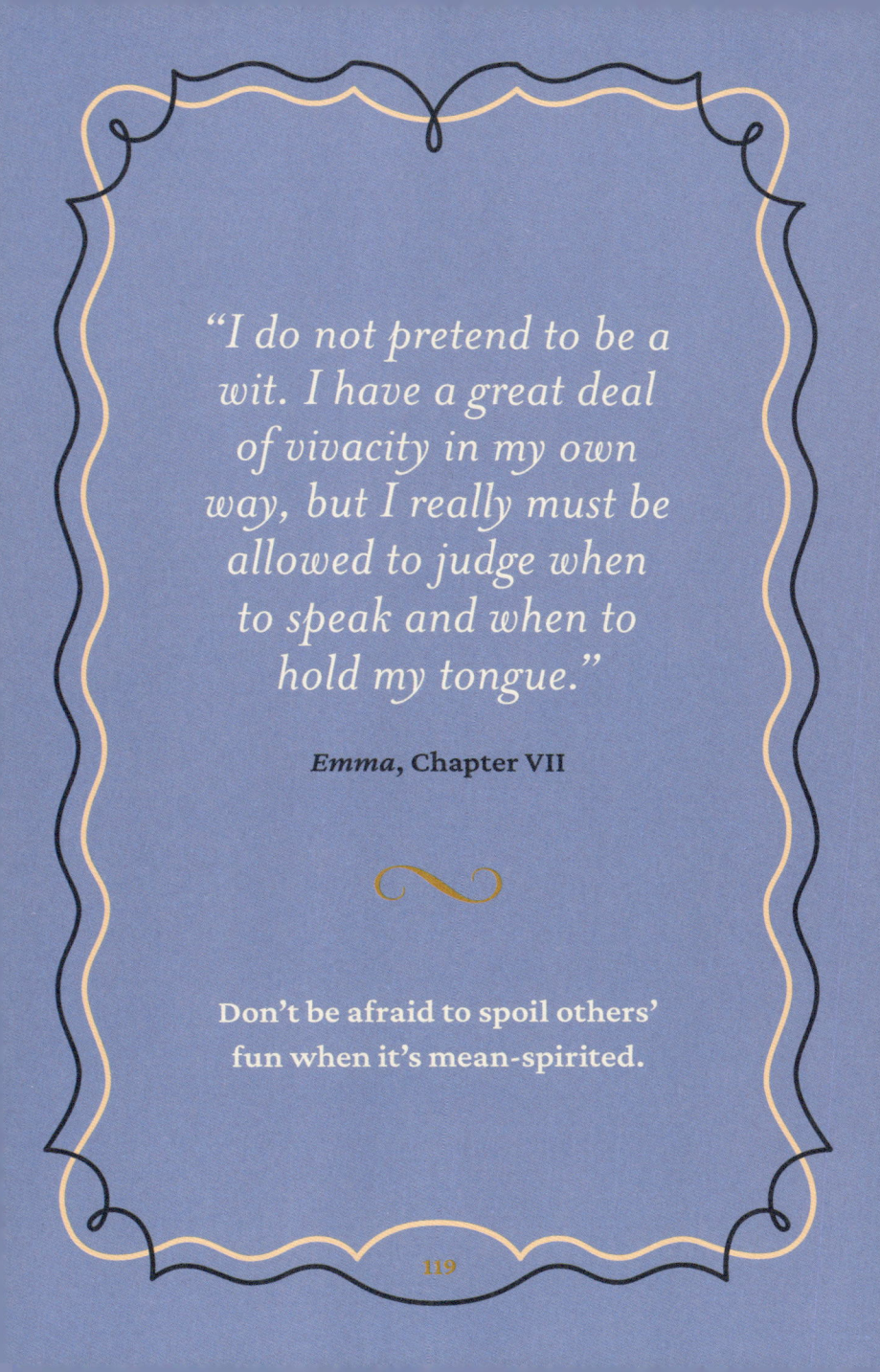

"I do not pretend to be a wit. I have a great deal of vivacity in my own way, but I really must be allowed to judge when to speak and when to hold my tongue."

Emma, Chapter VII

Don't be afraid to spoil others' fun when it's mean-spirited.

A ROMANTIC WHO ALMOST DIES FROM WET STOCKINGS

MARIANNE DASHWOOD

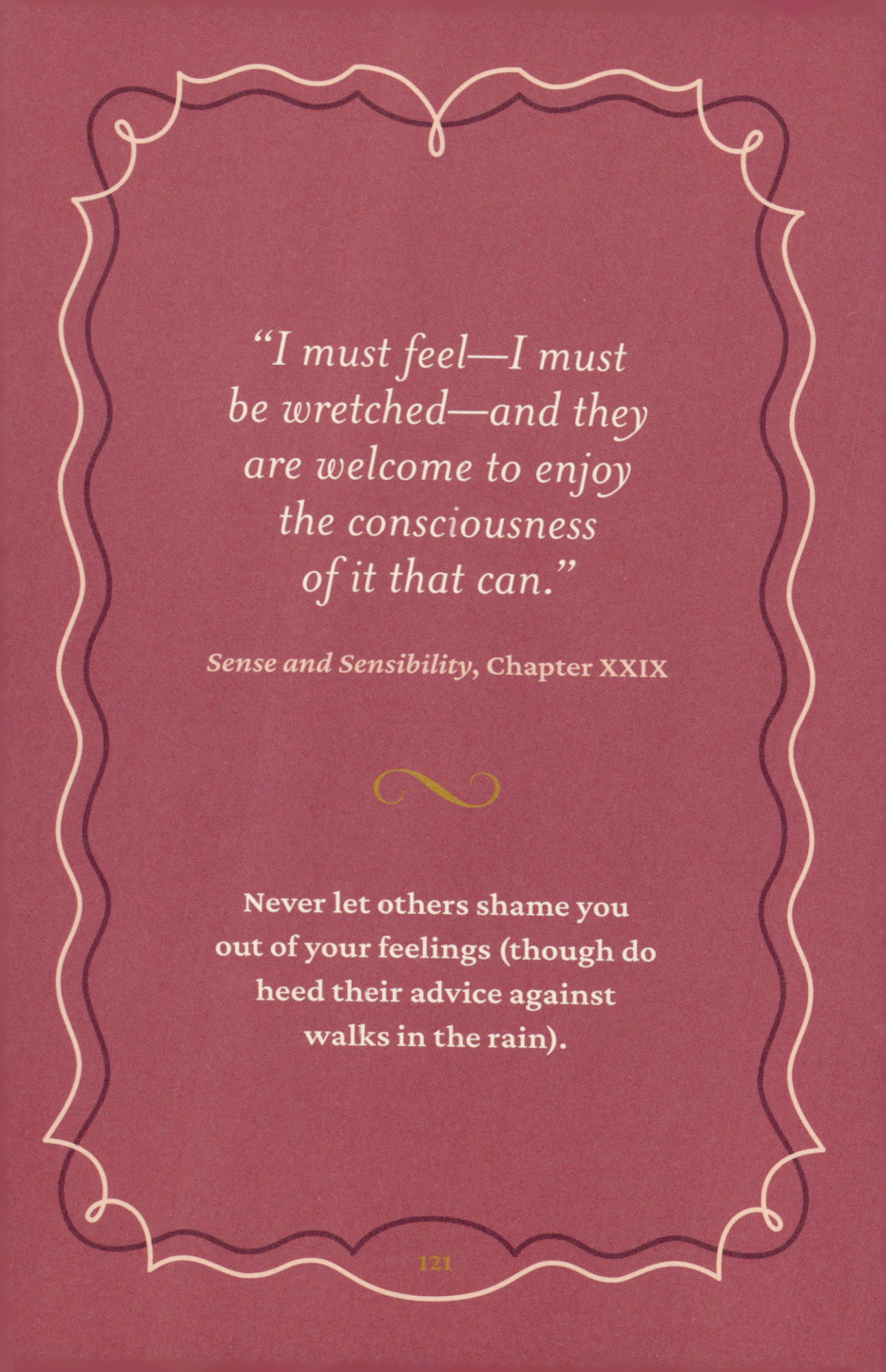

"I must feel—I must be wretched—and they are welcome to enjoy the consciousness of it that can."

Sense and Sensibility, Chapter XXIX

Never let others shame you out of your feelings (though do heed their advice against walks in the rain).

Must-have items to spend your pin money on

The cost of repairs to the estate's fences, taxes, and food for the whole household to live on: expenditures that are necessary, certainly, but not very interesting and matters for someone else. Time is better spent considering the small pleasures one can discover in town. On your next trip, look to purchase:

- An ornate fan with which to show off your face and/or hide it, depending on the needs of the evening and whether you are flirting with a gentleman, or pretending you didn't hear another's invitation to dance.

- The finest gown you can afford to show off all of your ... accomplishments.

- Ribbons and netting and lace to make that gown look fresh when you inevitably rewear it.

- Some more ribbons and netting and lace to make it look fresh all over again.

- Another ball? You will need *more* ribbons and netting and lace for that gown.

- Gloves and hair ornaments that will complement every version of your one gown.

- Something warm to wrap about your throat at night, to ease your mother's nerves.

- Novels, novels, and more novels. The person who collects novels collects the greatest powers of the human mind, despite what handsome clergymen may say.

- Very serious things to show you are a very serious person. A newspaper, perhaps, or some other plain object that will impress boring people, like clergymen.

- Some pins.

NARRATOR

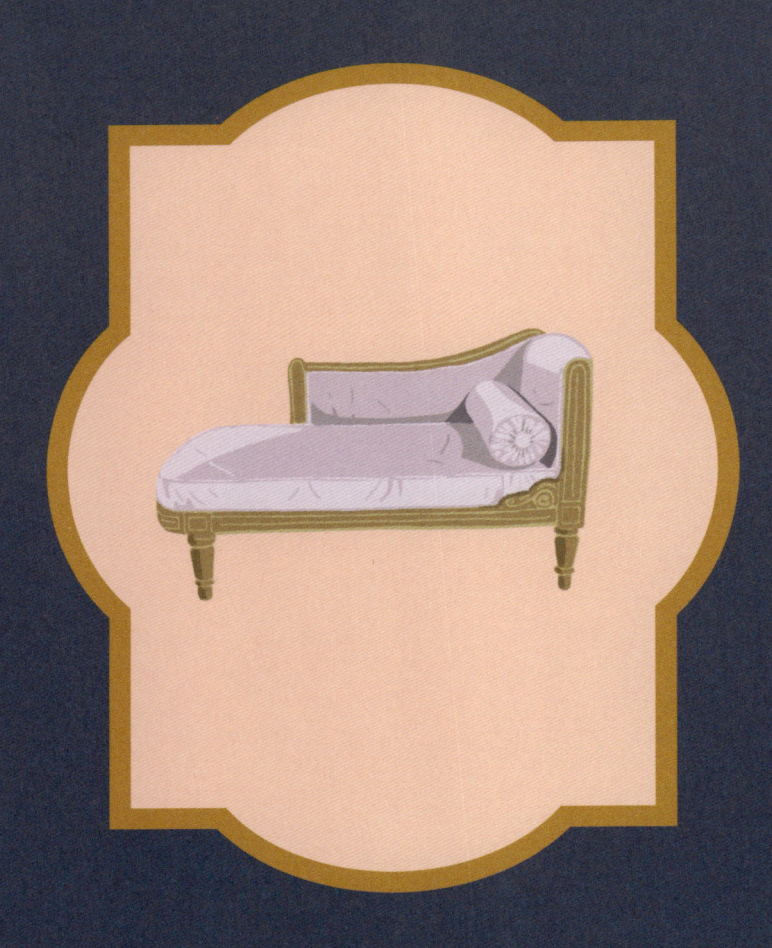

PERSUASION

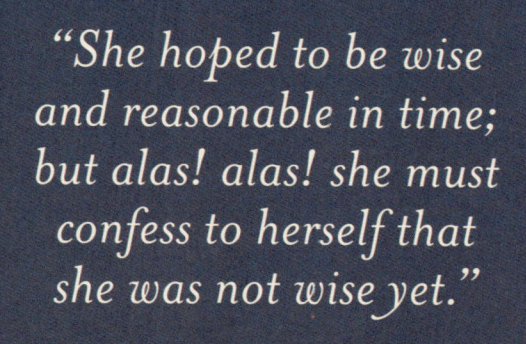

"*She hoped to be wise and reasonable in time; but alas! alas! she must confess to herself that she was not wise yet.*"

Persuasion, Chapter XIX

❦

While it may take longer than seven years to become wiser, you're unlikely to become any less charming.

THE DASHWOODS' SOURCE OF GOSSIP

Mrs Jennings

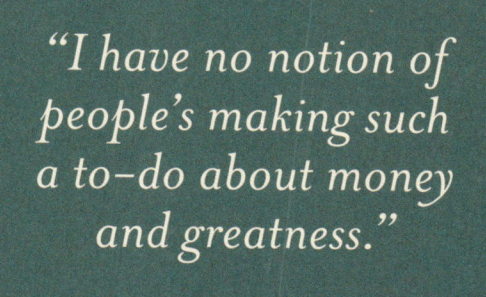

"I have no notion of people's making such a to-do about money and greatness."

Sense and Sensibility, Chapter XXXVII

∾

More carriages and fashionable dresses are always less impressive than genuine kindness and an open mind.

ANNE ELLIOT'S DASHING EX

CAPTAIN WENTWORTH

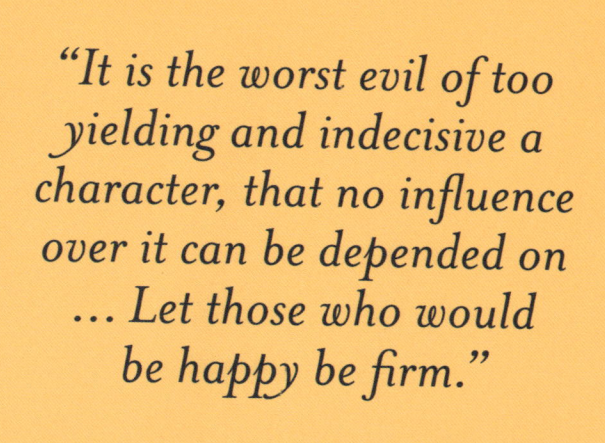

"It is the worst evil of too yielding and indecisive a character, that no influence over it can be depended on ... Let those who would be happy be firm."

Persuasion, **Chapter X**

∽

Heed advice but remain discerning in matters of real importance.

Hobbies That Are Better Than Matchmaking

Matchmaking is the best kind of hobby when you think you know better than everybody else and love to meddle. Which means it is also the perfect hobby if you want to displease every one of your acquaintances. As appealing as taking credit for an impeccable match may be, it is far safer to try one of these activities:

STRAWBERRY-PICKING

You could also try other fruits. Blueberries. Peaches. Maybe even a vegetable.

PORTRAIT PAINTING

Everyone has an artist within them. Somewhere. Even if it is buried very deep.

THEATRE

Producing, directing, acting ... it may be a little scandalous, but that only adds to the lark.

WALKING

Vigorous exercise is a must. Just be mindful of rain and muddying the hem of your dress.

TRAVEL

Perhaps, if you are lucky, you may see distant, mysterious lands like the village next to yours in as little as one day.

SHOPPING

The only downside is that you may end up with too many ribbons (and not enough money).

BALLS

Hosting them. Attending them. Dancing at them. Critiquing them. There is nothing like a good ball to occupy one's attention.

FALLING IN LOVE

You will never even think about other people's love lives if you have one of your own to worry about.

READING

It is very important to improve one's mind—and not sporadically.

WRITING

Matchmake characters of your own invention. It is the most rewarding type of matchmaking, because here, you do know better than everybody else and can exert complete control.

A WITTY MAN AND SOMEWHAT
USELESS FATHER

MR
BENNET

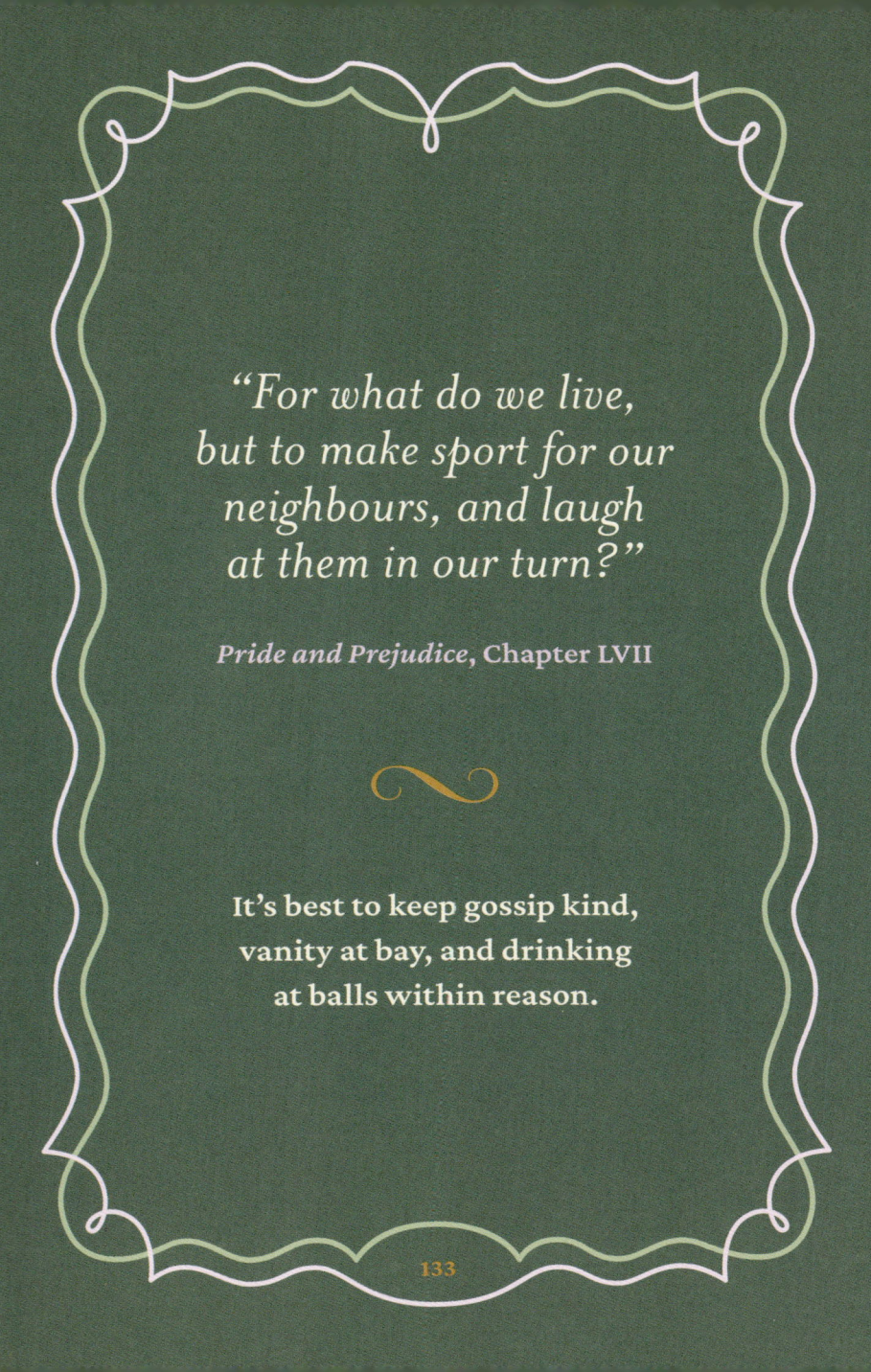

> *"For what do we live,
> but to make sport for our
> neighbours, and laugh
> at them in our turn?"*

Pride and Prejudice, Chapter LVII

It's best to keep gossip kind,
vanity at bay, and drinking
at balls within reason.

A HEROINE WITH GOOD INTENTIONS

Emma Woodhouse

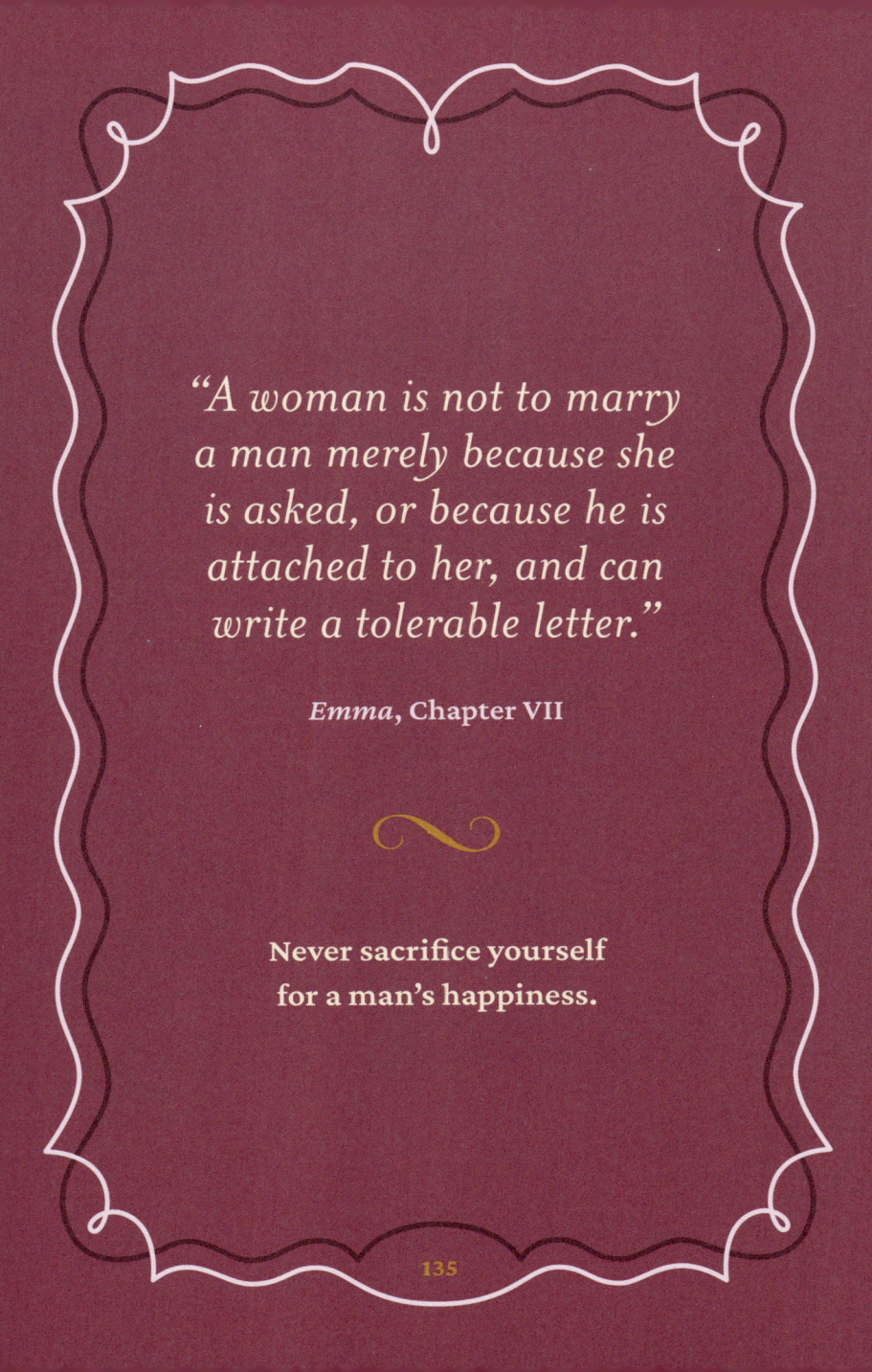

"A woman is not to marry a man merely because she is asked, or because he is attached to her, and can write a tolerable letter."

Emma, Chapter VII

Never sacrifice yourself for a man's happiness.

A WOMAN WHO KNOWS WHAT SHE'S ABOUT

LADY CATHERINE DE BOURGH

> "But however insincere you *may* choose to be, you shall not find me so. My character has ever been celebrated for its sincerity and frankness; and in a cause of such moment as this, I shall certainly not depart from it."

***Pride and Prejudice*, Chapter LVI**

Always stand up for what you believe in (even if it may backfire).

Truths that are Universally Acknowledged

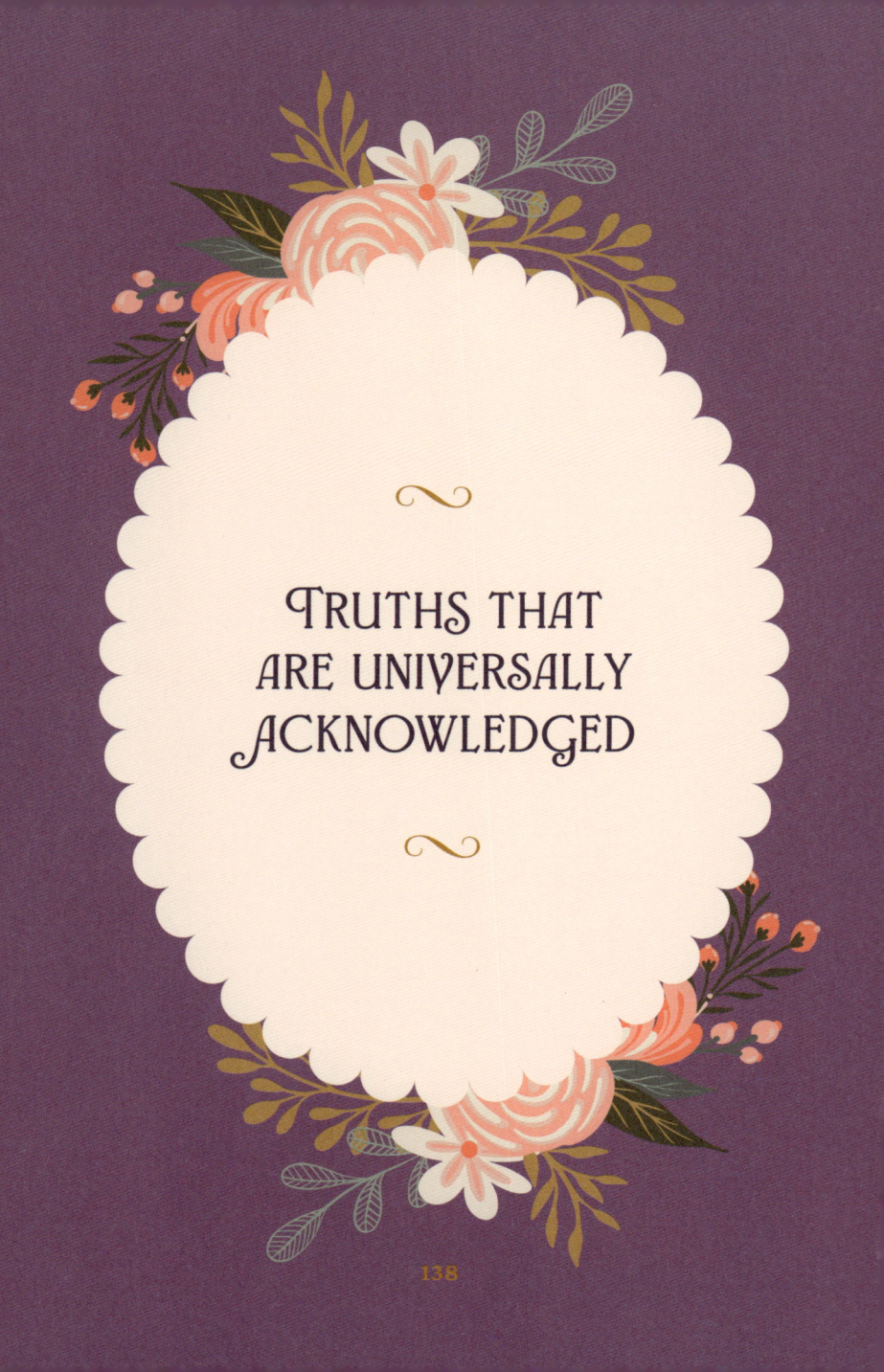

- If you think it will not rain, it will.

- If a gentleman seems too good to be true, he is.

- Your hair looks its best exactly one day before it is due to be trimmed.

- The contents of a shop window are never so interesting as when you are trying to avoid eye contact with a neighbour you do not wish to see.

- When struggling to sleep, turning your pillow over to the cold side will certainly help.

- A person who does not enjoy reading is a very dull person indeed.

- It is never easier to make friends than it is in the retiring room at the end of a long ball after several tumblers of punch.

- The more you love something or someone, the harder it is to talk about.

- There is nothing like cancelled plans for providing life's greatest reliefs.

- Unless it is removing one's stays at the end of the day.

- Removing one's stays after one's plans are cancelled is therefore the ultimate bliss.

- A single man in possession of a large fortune must be in want of a wife.

Smith Street Books

Published in 2025 by Smith Street Books
Naarm (Melbourne) | Australia
smithstreetbooks.com

ISBN: 978-1-9232-3901-2

All rights reserved. No part of this book may be reproduced or transmitted by any person or entity, in any form or by any means, electronic or mechanical, including photocopying, recording, scanning or by any storage and retrieval system, without the prior written permission of the publishers and copyright holders.

Smith Street Books respectfully acknowledges the Wurundjeri People of the Kulin Nation, who are the Traditional Owners of the land on which we work, and we pay our respects to their Elders past and present.

Copyright design © Smith Street Books

The moral right of the authors has been asserted.

Publisher: Hannah Koelmeyer
Editor: Avery Hayes
Text: Jenna Guillaume and Avery Hayes
Design concept and layout: Casey Schuurman
Illustrations: George Saad, Emi Chiba and Casey Schuurman
Proofreader: Pam Dunne

Text in this book previously appeared in *Austentatious*

Printed & bound in China by C&C Offset Printing Co., Ltd.

Book 376
10 9 8 7 6 5 4 3 2 1

MIX
Paper | Supporting responsible forestry
FSC® C008047